An Awareness of Language

JOEL B. MARGULIS

Forest Park Community College

WINTHROP PUBLISHERS, INC.

Cambridge, Massachusetts

Library of Congress Cataloging in Publication Data

Margulis, Joel B
   An awareness of language.

    1. Language and languages. I. Title.
P106.M34   808′.04275   74-34203
ISBN 0-87626-050-4

Copyright © 1975 by Winthrop Publishers, Inc.
17 Dunster Street, Cambridge, Massachusetts 02138

*This book is gratefully dedicated to
my Mother and Father*

Special Acknowledgment

*To Jill
without which nothing*

Contents

Preface

MAN: What's he got that I haven't got?
WOMAN: Awareness.
MAN: What's that?

—Mason Williams

The story is told that when Samuel Morse threw the switch that set in motion the first telegraph message, someone close by remarked with fascination that now it was possible for Maine to speak to Florida. When Ralph Waldo Emerson, miles away in Boston, heard of the remark, he was supposed to have asked flatly whether, indeed, Maine had anything to say to Florida.

That question has been asked many times since—always with good reason. If, in fact, there is something worth saying, how it is said must be a major concern, for how we are talking to one another is how we are treating one another. Too often our language works not for us but against us, and if our language has failed us, perhaps we have failed our language—to know it, to understand it, to use it fully.

Language . . . is the indispensable mechanism of human life. —S. I. Hayakawa

Learning about language is a way of making it work for us, and the concepts focused on in this book, although generally unrecognized, have been around for awhile. Becoming acquainted with them, it is hoped, will lead to an awareness of language and how to deal with it. I have tried to present a study of language using historical incidents, sheet music, cartoons, and advertisements. In our world few things happen in isolation (does anything?) and a statement, poem, short story, song, or work of art can serve as a useful point of departure.

The text itself, as well as the "Suggestions" and quoted material, is to be taken as not only the study of language but as sources for writing. Language is, after all, learned by using it in the freest and most open manner possible. And although I have no intention of telling anyone how to teach a class or use this book, I strongly recommend that the journal entry be the basis of student writing. Such entries carry a freshness and spontaneity that is too often stifled in the formal essay, and such freshness and spontaneity lead to the essentials—confidence and fluency. Writing seems best when it is restricted least.

. . . amid all the vastly developed means of communication that bombard us on all sides, actual personal communication is exceedingly difficult and rare. —Rollo May

In all our communication, we need to know about language—what it is and how it works. It is, in the poet's phrase, "too much with us,"

v

and we need to get a firmer grip. That firmer grip will take time and effort and awareness.

Only the question remains: are we going to bother?

PERSONAL ACKNOWLEDGMENTS

The depth of my gratitude goes to my friend and colleague, Dick Friedrich, whose talent and patience even beyond this book amounted to help I simply could not have done without.

I also wish to thank Elisabeth McPherson, whose suggestions led to numerous improvements, as did Greg Cowan's careful reading of the manuscript.

I am deeply indebted to Ron Estes and Jerry Garger, whose help over the years has been invaluable, as has my personal and professional relationship with each member of the English Department at Forest Park Community College: Jerry Brown, Adam Casmier, Mary Ann Cook, Greg Cowan, Jack Craig, Kathe Dunlop, Dick Friedrich, Jim Funkhouser, Alice Grant, Angela Harris, Jim Harris, Jim Hoelscher, Malkom Jackoway, Hattie Jackson, David Kuester, Elisabeth McPherson, Joe Salvia, Lynn Siegel, Larry Skinner, Sally Souder, and Alvie Watt.

I am certainly indebted to Joe Cosand, Ralph Lee, Bob Richey, Phil Carlock, and Fred Diaz for making Forest Park a rare and positive place.

The assistance I received from the Forest Park library staff, especially Mary Ann Mitchell, Carol Hess, Helen Hug, and JoEllen Flagg, was most helpful.

Especially kind with their superior art work were Tibor Nagy and Dennis Berner.

For their help in preparing the manuscript I want to thank Peggy Kelly, Joyce Wess, Pearl Brown, and especially Sheila Sayer.

I also want to thank Joyce and Arthur Margulis and Arthur Jr., Billy, Jimmy, Tommy; Pat and Dave Grossman, Robbie and Joey Flegel, Izzy and Herbie Palans, Suzy and Maury Jaffer, Lynn and Bill Selby, Emmy and Lowell Lukas, Mary Lou and Jim Miles, David Lacks, John Woods, John Moseley, Joel Allen, Sue Bentley, Vicki and Tony Previte, Charles Bell, and Robert Camp. And thanks, too, to Audrey Roth.

And sincere thanks go to Bob Sarnoff, whose understanding of the artistic process led to unstinting encouragement.

Finally, I wish to acknowledge the aid and tolerance of Paul O'Connell, Meg Dall, Sharon Bryan, and Barbara Sonnenschein of Winthrop Publishers.

Acknowledgments

Williams, Mason, Preface. From *The Mason Williams Reading Matter* by Mason Williams. Copyright © 1964, 1965, 1966, 1969 by Mason Williams. Used by permission of Doubleday & Company, Inc.

Hayakawa, S. I., Preface; pp. 19, 51, 84. From S. I. Hayakawa, *Language In Thought and Action*, Harcourt Brace Jovanovich, Inc. Reprinted by permission.

May, Rollo, Preface; pp. 19, 22–23. From Rollo May, *Love and Will*. Copyright © 1969 by W. W. Norton & Co., Inc., New York. With the permission of the publisher.

Johnson, Nicholas, pp. 1, 91–92. From *How To Talk Back to Your Television Set* by Nicholas Johnson. Little, Brown and Company in association with Atlantic Monthly Press, publishers.

Roosevelt, Theodore, p. 3. From *Winning the West* by Theodore Roosevelt. G. P. Putnam's Sons, copyright 1889, with permission of the publisher.

Myers, L. M., p. 4. From L. M. Myers, *American English*, New York, 1952. With permission of L. M. Myers.

Whorf, B. L., pp. 5, 78, 79, 80. From *Language, Thought, and Reality* by B. L. Whorf, by permission of the MIT Press, Cambridge, Massachusetts.

Davis, Ossie, p. 5. From "The English Language Is My Enemy!" by Ossie Davis, *Negro History Bulletin*, April 1967. Reprinted by permission of the *Negro History Bulletin*.

Hernandez, Aileen, pp. 5, 123. From "The Preening of America" by Aileen C. Hernandez. Reprinted from the Pasadena, California, *Star-News* with permission.

Todd, John H., p. 6ff. From "The Mysterious Language of the Sea" by John H. Todd, *The Lamp*, © 1973, Exxon Corporation. Reprinted by permission.

Lorenz, Konrad, pp. 6–7. From *King Solomon's Ring* by Konrad Lorenz, copyright © 1952 by Thomas Y. Crowell Co., Inc., with their permission.

Graham, Ellen, pp. 7–8. From "Smells and Behavior" by Ellen Graham. *The Wall Street Journal*, December 19, 1972. © 1972 Dow Jones & Company, Inc. All rights reserved.

Schofield, Michael, pp. 8–10. From "For a Lobster What's Vital is How Things —and Other Lobsters—Smell" by Michael Schofield. *Smithsonian* Magazine, August 1972. By permission of the editor, Edward K. Thompson.

Hall, Edward T., pp. 10, 15. Excerpt from *The Hidden Dimension* by E. T. Hall. Copyright © 1966 by E. T. Hall. Used by permission of Doubleday & Company, Inc.

Thorpe, E. H., pp. 11, 146. From "Duet-Singing Birds" by E. H. Thorpe. Copyright © 1973 by Scientific American, Inc. All rights reserved. Reprinted with permission.

Fox, Michael, p. 11. From Michael Fox, *Understanding Your Dog*, copyright © 1972 by Michael Fox. Coward, McCann & Geoghegan, Inc., publishers.

Evans, H. E., p. 11. From the book *Life On A Little-known Planet* by Howard E. Evans. Illustrated by Arnold Clapan. Copyright © 1968 by Howard E. Evans. Published by E. P. Dutton & Co., Inc., and used with their permission.

Lilly, John C., p. 13. Excerpts from *Mind of the Dolphin* by Lilly, J. Cunningham. Copyright © 1969. Used by permission of Doubleday & Company, Inc.

Premack, David, p. 14. Excerpted from *Psychology Today* Magazine, September 1970. Copyright © Ziff-Davis Publishing Company. Reprinted by permission.

Goodall, Jane, p. 15. From Jane van Lawick-Goodall, *In the Shadow of Man*, Houghton Mifflin Company. Reprinted with permission.

Langer, Suzanne, pp. 15–16, 18. From "The Lord of Creation" by Suzanne Langer. *Fortune*, January 1944. Reprinted courtesy of *Fortune* magazine.

Elsen, Albert, p. 21ff. From *Purposes of Art* by Albert Elsen, Holt, Rinehart and Winston, Inc., publisher. Used with permission.

Willett, Frank, p. 21n. From *African Art: An Introduction* by Frank Willett. © 1971 by Frank Willett. Reprinted by permission of Praeger Publishers, Inc., New York.

Trowell, Margaret, p. 22. From Margaret Trowell and Hans Nevermann, *African and Oceanic Art*, 1967, published by Harry N. Abrams, Inc., New York. Reprinted with permission.

Griesinger, G. A., p. 23. From G. A. Griesinger, *Joseph Haydn: Eighteenth-Century Gentleman and Genius*, University of Wisconsin Press. Reprinted with permission.

Condon, John C., p. 24. From John C. Condon, Jr., *Semantics and Communications*, New York: The Macmillan Company. Copyright © 1966 by John C. Condon, Jr. Reprinted by permission of the publisher.

de la Croix, Horst, and Tansey, Richard G., pp. 24, 26. From Gardner's *Art Through the Ages* by Horst de la Croix and Richard G. Tansey. Harcourt Brace Jovanovich, Inc., publishers. Reprinted with permission.

Hunter, Sam, pp. 24–25. From Sam Hunter, *American Art of the 20th Century*, 1973, Harry N. Abrams, Inc., New York, N.Y. Reprinted with permission.

Warhol, Andy, p. 27. From "What Is Pop Art?" by G. R. Swenson, *Art News*, November 1963. © ARTnews Associates 1963.

Hamilton, G. H., p. 28. From George Heard Hamilton, *19th and 20th Century Art*, Harry N. Abrams, Inc., New York, N.Y. Reprinted by permission.

Jackson, Arthur, and V. B., pp. 28–30. Reprinted from *The Me Nobody Knows*, ed. by Stephen M. Joseph, by arrangement with Avon Books. Copyright © 1969 by Stephen M. Joseph.

"Eleanor Rigby," p. 31. By Lennon/McCartney. Copyright © 1966 Northern Songs Ltd. "Imagine," p. 32. By John Lennon. Copyright © 1971 Northern Songs Ltd. All rights for the USA, its territories and possessions, and Canada controlled by Maclen Music, Inc., care of ATV Music Group. Used by permission. All rights reserved.

Roberts, Paul, p. 33. From the "Foreword" by Paul Roberts in *A Linguistic Reader*, edited by Graham Wilson, Harper & Row, Inc., 1967. Reprinted with permission.

Pei, Mario, p. 35. From *The Story of Language* by Mario Pei. Copyright © 1965, 1949 by Mario Pei. Reprinted by permission of J. B. Lippincott Company.

Chase, Stuart, pp. 36, 82, 83, 89. From "How Language Shapes Our Thoughts," copyright 1954 by Stuart Chase. Reprinted by permission of A. Watkins, Inc.

Gregory, Dick, pp. 38–9. From *The Shadow That Scares Me* by Dick Gregory.

Copyright © 1968 by Dick Gregory. Used by permission of Doubleday & Company, Inc.

Brautigan, Richard, p. 39. " 'Star-Spangled' Nails" from *The Pill Versus the Springhill Mine Disaster* by Richard Brautigan. Copyright © 1968 by Richard Brautigan. Reprinted by permission of Seymour Lawrence/Delacorte Press.

Johnson, Wendell, pp. 44, 83. From Wendell Johnson, *People In Quandries*, Harper & Row, Publishers, Inc. Reprinted with permission.

Schwartz, Donald, pp. 48–50. Reprinted from *ETC.: A Review of General Semantics* by permission of The International Society for General Semantics.

Trumbo, Dalton, p. 53. From *Johnny Got His Gun*, copyright © 1970 by Dalton Trumbo, Lyle Stuart, 1970. Reprinted by permission.

Chase, Stuart, pp. 53–4. From Stuart Chase, *The Tyranny of Words*, Harcourt Brace Jovanovich, Inc., publisher. Reprinted by permission.

Landers, Ann, pp. 55–6. Courtesy, Ann Landers, Publishers-Hall Syndicate, and the St. Louis *Post-Dispatch*.

Lippmann, Walter, pp. 56, 58. From Walter Lippmann, *Public Opinion*, The Macmillan Company, New York. Copyright © 1965 by Walter Lippmann. Used with permission.

Rapoport, Anatol, p. 56. Reprinted from *ETC.: A Review of General Semantics* by permission of The International Society for General Semantics.

Bardwick, Judith, pp. 57, 124. Reprinted from "Women's Liberation—Nice Idea, But It Won't Be Easy," *Psychology Today* Magazine, May 1973. Copyright © Ziff-Davis Publishing Company.

Scott, J. F., and Scott, L. H., p. 58. From *Prejudice and Race Relations*. Edited by Raymond W. Mack, copyright 1970 by The New York Times Company. Used by permission of the publisher.

Grier, W. H., and Cobbs, P. M., pp. 58–9. From *Black Rage* by William H. Grier and Price M. Cobbs, Basic Books, 1968. Reprinted with permission of the publisher.

Tuchman, Barbara, p. 59. From *Stilwell and the American Experience In China* by Barbara W. Tuchman. Copyright © 1970, 1971 by Barbara W. Tuchman. Reprinted with permission of the Macmillan Company.

Mayni, Carmen, p. 59. From "Women's Champion In A Strategic Post" by Ilene Barth. *Parade* Magazine, August 12, 1973. Reprinted by permission.

Harris poll, p. 59. Courtesy, St. Louis *Post-Dispatch*.

Hughes, Langston, pp. 59–61. "Coffee Break" from *Simple's Uncle Sam* by Langston Hughes, copyright © 1965 by Langston Hughes. Reprinted with the permission of Farrar, Straus & Giroux, Inc.

Lee, Irving J., p. 62. Reprinted from *ETC.: A Review of General Semantics* by permission of The International Society for General Semantics.

O'Brien, Patricia, pp. 62–3. Reprinted by permission of Quadrangle/The New York Times Book Co. from *The Woman Alone* by Patricia O'Brien. Copyright © 1973 by Patricia O'Brien Koval.

Mencken, H. L., pp. 62, 93. From *Mencken* by Carl Bode, Southern Illinois University Press, copyright © 1969 by Carl Bode.

Brown, Dee, p. 63. From *Bury My Heart At Wounded Knee* by Dee Brown. Holt, Rinehart and Winston, Inc., publishers. Reprinted with permission.

Hitler, Adolf, p. 63. From *Mein Kampf*, translated by Ralph Manheim, Houghton Mifflin Company, publishers. Reprinted with permission.

Asimov, Isaac, pp. 63–4. From the book *The Sensuous Dirty Old Man* by Isaac

Asimov. Published by Walker & Co., New York. Copyright © by Isaac Asimov.

Kluckhohn, Clyde, pp. 64, 81. From *Mirror For Man* by Clyde Kluckhohn. Copyright 1949 by McGraw-Hill, Inc. Used with permission of McGraw-Hill Book Company.

Kanfer, Stefan, p. 69. From "Words From Watergate" by Stefan Kanfer. Reprinted by permission from TIME, The Weekly Newsmagazine; copyright Time Inc.

Mintz, Harold K., pp. 70–71. "Playing With Words" from *The Quill*. Reprinted by permission of the Editor, Charles Long.

TIME magazine, p. 73. From "Leaving the Quagmire." Reprinted by permission from TIME, The Weekly Newsmagazine; copyright Time Inc.

Funkhouser, James, p. 74. From James Funkhouser, "A Various Standard," *College English*, March 1973. Reprinted with the permission of NCTE and the author.

Scott, Fred Newton, p. 75. From Fred Newton Scott, "Standard of American Speech," *English Journal*, January 1917. Reprinted with the permission of NCTE.

McPherson, Elisabeth, p. 75. From "Language Learning: The Desert of Ignorance," courtesy Elisabeth McPherson.

Stanford, Barbara Dodds, p. 76. From "Is Teaching Grammar Immoral?" by Barbara Dodds Stanford. Reprinted from *Changing Education*, official publication of the American Federation of Teachers, AFL-CIO, Spring 1970. Reprinted with permission.

Kluckhohn, Clyde, and Leighton, Dorothea, pp. 77, 81. From Clyde Kluckhohn and Dorothea Leighton, *The Navaho*, Harvard University Press, 1962. Reprinted with permission.

Chase, Stuart, p. 78. Reprinted from the "Foreword," *Language, Thought and Reality* by Benjamin Lee Whorf, by permission of the MIT Press, Cambridge, Massachusetts.

Thomas, Lewis, pp. 79–80. From *The Lives of a Cell* by Lewis Thomas. Copyright © 1974 by Lewis Thomas. Reprinted by permission of The Viking Press, Inc.

Langacker, Ronald, p. 81. From Ronald Langacker, *Language and Its Structure*, Harcourt Brace Jovanovich, Inc., publisher. Reprinted with permission.

Albers, Josef, p. 83. From Josef Albers, *Interaction of Color* (Yale University Press, New Haven, 1971), p. 3. Reprinted with permission.

Fabun, Don, pp. 83, 88. From *Three Roads to Awareness* by Don Fabun. Published by Glencoe Press. Reprinted with permission.

St. Louis *Post-Dispatch*, pp. 86, 104, 122. Courtesy, St. Louis *Post-Dispatch*.

Daniels, Roger, p. 87. From Roger Daniels, *Concentration Camps USA*, Holt, Rinehart and Winston, Inc., publishers. Reprinted with permission.

Lenin, Nikolai, pp. 87–8. From Robert Payne, *The Life and Death of Lenin*, Simon & Schuster with Avon Books, publishers. Reprinted by permission.

Seng T'san, p. 90. From "Trust and the Heart" by Seng T'san in *Buddhist Texts Through the Ages*, E. Conze, ed. Reprinted with permission of Philosophical Library, Inc., publishers.

Baker, S. S., pp. 91, 92, 112. From *The Permissible Lie* by Samm Sinclair Baker. Reprinted by permission of Collins-Knowlton-Wing, Inc. Copyright © 1968 by Samm Sinclair Baker.

Miller, Clyde, pp. 92, 95. From "How to Detect Propaganda." In *A Complete Course in Freshman English* by Harry Shaw.

Payne, Robert, p. 92. From Robert Payne, *The Life and Death of Adolf Hitler,* copyright © 1973, Praeger Publishers, Inc. Reprinted with permission.

Ruch, F. L., and Zimbardo, P. G., p. 93. From Floyd L. Ruch and Philip G. Zimbardo, *Psychology and Life,* 8th edition. Copyright © 1971 by Scott, Foresman and Company. Reprinted by permission of the publisher.

Callahan, Daniel, pp. 93, 95, 98. From *Abortion: Law, Choice, and Morality* by Daniel Callahan. Copyright © 1970 by Daniel Callahan. Reprinted by permission of the Macmillan Company, Inc.

Newsweek, p. 93. From *Newsweek,* January 15, 1973. Copyright Newsweek, Inc. 1973, reprinted by permission.

Schlafly, Phyllis, p. 95. Copyright © 1973 by The New York Times Company. Reprinted by permission.

St. John, Jacqueline, p. 95. Reprinted by permission of "Vital Speeches of the Day," 38:528–32, June 15, 1972.

Embler, Weller, pp. 96, 105. Reprinted from *ETC.: A Review of General Semantics* by permission of the International Society for General Semantics.

Cooke, Alistair, pp. 96, 109, 113. From *Alistair Cooke's America.* Copyright © 1973 by Alistair Cooke. Reprinted by permission of Alfred A. Knopf, Inc.

Massie, Robert K., p. 100. From *Nicholas and Alexandra* by Robert K. Massie. Copyright © 1967 by Robert K. Massie. Reprinted by permission of Atheneum Publishers.

Huff, Darrell, pp. 100–101. From *How To Lie With Statistics* by Darrell Huff. Reprinted by permission of W. W. Norton & Company, Inc.

Plimpton, George, p. 101. From *Paper Lion* by George Plimpton, 1973, Harper & Row, Publishers, Inc. Reprinted with permission.

Ruby, Lionel, pp. 102, 105, 111. From *The Art of Making Sense,* 2nd edition, by Lionel Ruby. Reprinted by permission of the publisher, J. B. Lippincott Company. Copyright © 1968.

Landers, Ann, pp. 102–3. Courtesy, Ann Landers, Publishers-Hall Syndicate, and the Washington *Post.*

Goldston, Robert, p. 105. From *The Russian Revolution,* copyright © 1966, by Robert Goldston. Reprinted by permission of the publisher, The Bobbs-Merrill Company, Inc.

Halberstam, David, pp. 105–6. From *The Best and the Brightest* by David Halberstam. Copyright © 1969, 1971, 1972 by David Halberstam. Reprinted by permission of Random House, Inc.

Sunoco, p. 116. Courtesy Sun Oil Company.

Komisar, Lucy, pp. 119–21, 124. From *The New Feminism,* copyright © 1971 by Lucy Komisar. Used by permission of Franklin Watts, Inc.

Heide, Wilma Scott, pp. 121, 122–3. Reprinted by permission of "Vital Speeches of the Day," 38:403–9, April 15, 1972.

"Dick and Jane As Victims," pp. 120–22. From *Dick and Jane As Victims: Sex Stereotyping in Children's Readers.* Women on Words and Images. P.O. Box 2163, Princeton, N.J. 08540.

Sutton, William A., pp. 124–5. Reprinted courtesy of the author, William A. Sutton, Department of English, Ball State University, Muncie, Indiana 47306. 1973.

Knowles, Louis L., and Prewitt, Kenneth, pp. 126–8. From Louis L. Knowles and Kenneth Prewitt, eds., *Institutional Racism in America,* © 1969, by permission of Prentice-Hall, Inc., Englewood Cliffs, New Jersey.

Acknowledgments

Bosmajian, Haig A., pp. 128–135. "The Language of White Racism" from *College English*, December 1969. Copyright © 1969 by The National Council of Teachers of English. Reprinted by permission of the publisher and the author.

Barth, John, p. 143. Excerpt from *The Floating Opera* by John Barth. Copyright © 1956, 1967 by John Barth. Used by permission of Doubleday & Company, Inc.

Tuchman, Barbara, p. 144. From *The Guns of August* by Barbara W. Tuchman. Copyright © 1962 by Barbara W. Tuchman. Reprinted by permission of the Macmillan Company, Inc.

Baldwin, James, p. 145. From "Sonny's Blues" by James Baldwin. Copyright © 1957 by James Baldwin. Reprinted from *Going to Meet the Man* by James Baldwin by permission of the publisher, The Dial Press. First published in *Partisan Review*.

Rosenbaum, Jean, p. 146. Reprinted by permission of Hawthorn Books, Inc. from *Is Your Volkswagen a Sex Symbol?* Copyright © 1972 by Jean Rosenbaum. All rights reserved.

Packard, Vance, p. 147. Copyright © 1957 by Vance Packard. From the book *The Hidden Persuaders* by Vance Packard. Published by David McKay Company, Inc. Used with permission.

1 What Language Is

AN OVERVIEW

Not much is known about the origin of language. Evidence suggests that humans' earliest writing began about 5,000 years ago, but of course they were speaking long before that. They have, in fact, always been speakers before writers.

Even today, not enough is known about how children learn quite early in life to master the basics of their native language, but by the time they enter classrooms for the first time, usually at age five, they are already quite proficient at speaking. We think of them going off to school to learn to read and write, not to learn to speak. Precisely how quickly children have advanced from the prelanguage (babbling) stage to the more sophisticated levels of oral communication varies with the individual, but by age seven or eight, they can pretty well hold their own in almost any conversation.

Yet at the same age most children have hardly begun to write, and writing is not the same as speaking—a distinction that initially seems so elementary, so obvious, as to be useless. Yet in spite of its simplicity, perhaps because of it, it continues to go unnoticed, as do many other things. Also unnoticed is the fact that though students may enter school "information-rich" (thanks to the mass media) they can still come out "communication-poor," and since knowledge about language continues to be poorly and inaccurately taught, they'll be joining most of the rest of us, who won't be consciously aware of several important things about language:

By the time the average child enters kindergarten he has already spent more hours learning about his world from television than the hours he would spend in a college classroom earning a B.A. degree.
—*Nicholas Johnson*

that our language is made up of *symbols*.

that a *symbol* is something that represents something else.

that our *spoken language* is made up of sounds that *symbolize* (stand for) certain things that exist in the world around us, such as the sound we make when we say the word "car."

1

that our *written language* is made up of what we call *letters*, which *symbolize* (stand for) the sounds we make. For example, the letters "c" and "a" and "r" when written side by side, in this order, represent the sound we made above when we said "car."

that the relationship is *arbitrary* between the sounds we make and the things we mean, or between the letters we write and the sounds we make. That whatever relationships exist between these various means of communication do so by agreement among people. For instance, no one I know who hears the sound "car" has a picture in his mind of a "crocodile." But, if we had agreed on the sound "crocodile" instead of on the sound "car," we'd be driving around polluting the air in our 6- and 8-cylinder, 4-wheeled "crocodiles."

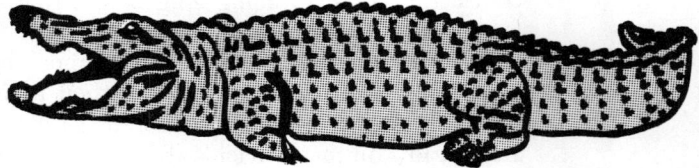

Courtesy, Tibor Nagy

I wouldn't want to drive one of these!

that we have a *silent language* which involves neither sounds nor letters, but which communicates quite accurately through the body language of *gestures* and *facial expressions*. Often these gestures and expressions accompany vocal messages: We say "hello" as we nod our head, wave our hand as we say "goodby." This combination can reassure the sender that his message has been more clearly understood. But in particular circumstances, the eyes can say it all. A look from Humphrey Bogart tells us everything we need to know. Nor is the power of silence alone to be underestimated. Responding to someone's adamant argument with total silence can often have surprising results. Try it sometime—but beware.

What we have thus far formed is a good working basis for an understanding of language, but there are other essential aspects that need looking into. Here are some of them:

that not all our words are as easily defined as "car" or

"crocodile." Some words are *specific* and *concrete*; others are *vague* and *abstract*. Will one definition of "patriotism" suffice for all Americans in the coming months and years as the question of amnesty remains an issue? Our language, then, has *levels of abstraction* and we'll be dealing with these different levels.

that these levels of abstraction give us *classification,* one of our most useful tools, and *stereotyping,* one of our most abused tools of communication. *Classification* is the process of gathering things that are similar. It is a matter of great convenience, since we cannot give a separate name to every item in the universe. We could hardly communicate (know what someone else is referring to) without being able to talk about "cars" or even "Chevrolets" or "Fords." Nor could we speak about "pets" or even about "dogs" and "cats." *Classification* is indispensable to communication, with the classifier himself determining which characteristics

*This great continent could not have been kept as nothing but a game preserve for squalid savages.
—Theodore Roosevelt, speaking about the Indian Americans.*

of similar items he wishes to consider. *Stereotyping,*
however, ignores essential differences. It fails to see
individuals as individuals, irresponsibly lumping together people who may have one and only one matching characteristic, such as skin color, income, or political party. *Stereotyping*—by all of us—is as plentiful
as it is ignorant.

that certain words may be taken by us on the level of *denotation,* a word's literal, or dictionary definition; or
on the level of *connotation,* the emotional reaction to
the word itself. For example, the *denotative* meaning
for a certain household pet—"a domesticated carni-
vore, *Felis domestica* or *F. catus,* bred in a number of
varieties"—will change little from dictionary to dictionary. But from person to person, the *connotative*
meaning of the word will vary greatly, as each one
brings different experiences, feelings, and associations
to this same animal, a "cat." So while Snoopy's reaction is understandable—at least on the instinctive
level of any proud and distinguished beagle—a similar
reaction by some humans to just the *word itself* remains one of the mysterious aspects of the power of
language (as well as an example of the failure to separate a word from the thing it stands for).

that in fact, our search for pleasant connotation leads
often to *euphemism,* the attempt to make the unpleasant sound pleasant. To use a couple of common
examples, people don't die, they "pass away." People
don't have syphilis or gonorrhea, they have "social
diseases." And while we are only now beginning in
this last instance to deal with *euphemism* and its
danger of allowing people to ignore reality, it—like
the two diseases mentioned—is rampant in a modern
society.

that there are variations of the same language called *dialects,* which are differences in the sounds we make, the
words we choose, and the ways in which we put those
words together to form phrases and sentences. The
provincial Frenchman who does not speak Parisian
French or the American blacks, for example, who do
not speak the so-called "prestige" or "standard" English suffer from the *value judgments* of people who

fail to see dialect as simply a *different* (rather than an "inferior" or "superior") way of speaking the same language. As an unfortunate result, *dialect* has unjustified but nevertheless powerful social, political, and economic ramifications.

that no language is capable of saying everything about anything, especially in the area of inner thoughts and feelings. We can do little more than approximate one another's experiences. But . . .

that our language may influence the way we think and the way we view the world around us, with different cultures seeing the world differently.

that our language is neither so rigid or inflexible as we are often led to believe. Language loses its greatest potential if we forget that "maybe" exists between "yes" and "no," and if we forget that shades of "gray" exist between "black" and "white."

that often words are effectively—even expertly—misused by those who wish to serve their own ends. Not all attempts to direct people's thinking are made for the wrong reasons (depending on one's point of view), but we need a keen awareness of the appeals and techniques used in *persuasion* and *propaganda,* and errors made in thinking which account for logical fallacies.

that in our own culture, a portion of our language is *racist,* another is *sexist,* and both strongly influence our attitudes.

that *order*—the particular arrangement of ideas in a piece of writing—occurs usually in one of two ways: it is *imposed* beforehand on what is going to be written, or it is *natural* to the material, growing out of what has already been written.

This is a brief glimpse, an overview, of what our language is, how it works and what is involved in its use, and we'll be taking a closer look at each of these aspects. I suppose it's just human nature to take for granted precisely those things we need to be most aware of. But I think we can already draw certain fundamental conclusions: words don't exist by themselves, they are not magic (though they sometimes seem to be); they mean only what people mean, whether it is the speaker (writer) who sends them or the listener (reader) who receives them. While arguments about who created humans may go on endlessly, there is little doubt as to who created words. The problem, simply stated, is humans' lack of a clear understanding of the vehicles of their communication, whether the vehicle is spoken, written, or silent.

COMMUNICATION AMONG NONHUMANS: THE SIGN AT THE CENTER

All this, by the way, is not to suggest that humans alone of the earth's creatures have complex means of communication. As Dr. John H. Todd, an assistant researcher at the Woods Hole Oceanographic Institute in Massachusetts has pointed out, "Communication is essential to life. It is the means by which plants and animals make known to their own kind, to friends or foes, who they are and what they are doing. This is true for almost all living things, down to simple marine bacteria." And as Dutch-born biologist Jella Atema, also of the Institute at Woods Hole has explained, "For us, as humans, vision is most important in the process of communication. Our thinking is most affected by seeing and hearing. Smell and taste are less developed." For many other animals, however, this is not the case, according to Dr. Atema. "Take a dog. How does it know when you're scared? It doesn't see very well, but it can smell your chemical 'aura.' Some animals are even more nonvisual or use entirely different sensory systems." And Dr. Todd makes this major point: "Since the 'languages' of animals are the means by which they organize their lives in relation to each other—just as do humans —communication is crucial to their survival." How our nonhuman fellow inhabitants do the job is worth investigating, however briefly. Making comparisons and contrasts will help us better understand our own communication process.

Body language, for instance, is used throughout the animal kingdom. For example, when fighting-fish approach one another, explains scientist Konrad Lorenz in *King Solomon's Ring,*

> they begin gradually to light up in all their incandescent glory. The glow pervades their bodies almost as quickly as the wire of an electric heater grows red. The fins unfold themselves like ornamental fans. . . . And now follows a dance of burning passion, a dance which is not play but real earnest, a dance of life or death, of be-all or end-all. To begin with, strangely enough, it is uncertain whether it will lead to love overtures and mating, or whether it will develop, by an equally flowing transition, into a bloody battle. Fighting fish recognize the sex of members of

their own species not simply by seeing it but by watching the way in which it responds to the severely ritualized, inherited, instinctive movements of the dancer.

The meeting of two previously unacquainted fighting-fish begins with a mutual "showing off," a swaggering act of self-display in which every luminous colour-spot and every iridescent ray of the wonderful fins is brought into maximum play. Before the glorious male, the modestly garbed female lowers the flag—by folding her fins—and, if she is unwilling to mate, flees immediately. Should she be willing to mate, she approaches the male with shy insinuating movements, that is to say, in an attitude directly opposed to that of the swaggering male. And now begins a love ceremonial which, if it cannot compare in grandeur with the male war-dance, can emulate it in grace of movement.

The war-dance that occurs when two male fighting-fish meet face-to-face will often end in death for one of them. The battle, if it occurs, is fierce. "The self-display-dance can last for hours but, should it develop into action, it is often only a matter of minutes before one of the combatants lies mortally wounded on the bottom."

Facial expressions, widely used by humans, are an effective way of sending and receiving messages even for wolves (who have at least fourteen different expressions) and for chimpanzees (who have at least sixteen). Seeing a dog's tail wag or seeing it tucked between a pair of hind legs (body language) combined with a grin or with a snarl (facial expressions) is communication enough for other canines and for humans to distinguish an invitation from a warning.

Even odors as means of communication serve extremely important social and biological functions not only for canines but for insects—who make up 4/5 of the animal world—and fish as well. Worker ants, for example, lead the others to food by leaving scent trails, little spots deposited along the way, by touching their abdomens to the ground as they move. And as Ellen Graham of the *Wall Street Jour-*

Courtesy, Tibor Nagy

"Tasty! Very tasty indeed!"

nal has reported, dead ants give off a chemical message that signals others to dispose of the body. "When daubed [by scientists] on an ant that's alive and kicking, the [odor of the chemical] still compels his mates to dutifully dump him on their trash heap outside the nest. He may resist and scramble back home, but until the [chemical] evaporates he'll be carted back again and again to the burial heap." In one species of the common fruit fly, courting and mating are carried on by the male's ability to taste the female of his species through sense organs located at the tips of his legs.

Dr. John Todd, for one, is fascinated by "the social bonds that exist between marine animals and the communication that sustains them." He discovered several years ago that some species of fish communicate by means of chemicals. "These fish are able to detect their own species, mates, enemies, the sex and status of others and even recognize individuals by chemical clues alone." Recent experiments at the Oceanographic Institute, investigating odor responses in aquatic animals, has determined that the nose is the means by which catfish carry on social communication, identifying one another, recognizing and remembering the odor of a bigger and more dangerous fish. As Michael Schofield reported in the *Smithsonian* Magazine (August 1972), after talking to Drs. John Todd, Laurie Stein, and Jella Atema, the "whiskers on a catfish are densely packed with taste buds from which nerves carry information to the brain. The continuous flow of water over the gills also reaches these taste buds so that the fish is constantly aware of the complete chemical composition of its environment." Dr. Atema detailed his findings in the following 1973 interview broadcast with a member of the American Chemical Society:

ACS MEMBER: One morning awhile back, Dr. Jella Atema, a young biologist studying how aquatic animals communicate, entered his laboratory to begin an experiment. In making preparations the day before, he put a number of small catfish into a tank. During the night most of the fish jumped out and died on the floor. Two of the small catfish, however, had landed in a neighboring tank. Much to the chagrin of the new arrivals the tank was already occupied by a huge catfish that had been in the lab for several years . . . and the larger fish gave them a terrible mauling. But catfish, as any youngster experienced with hook and line knows, can take quite a beating before they die.

ATEMA: So taking a chance we put them back in a tank,

the two of them, being beat up as they were, and
. . . they recovered, swimming around, and over
a few weeks time they even set up territories
[areas—land, water, or air—staked out and de-
fended by an animal against other members of
the same species], also like good catfish. . . .
They had two shelters, one on the left side and
one on the right side, and one fish was in one,
and one fish was in the other. Then we picked
up some water from the tank of the big mon-
strous catfish. We poured it into the tank of the
two territorial residents, and for about half a
minute nothing happened, and then presumably
when the water had penetrated to their area—
they started moving frantically around ducking
on the ground, and finally one fish ended up in
the part of the other fish together with the resident of that other part. The two were sitting together, clumping, huddling together. This was a
very dramatic example where the fish had remembered—in this case over a two week period
—the odor of the fish that had beaten them up,
very badly. We kept repeating this experiment
for up to two to three months, and the same reaction could be obtained after that long a time.

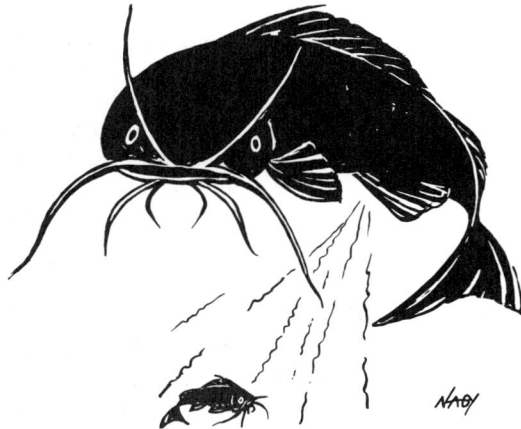

Courtesy, Tibor Nagy

"I can smell right away that I don't
want to tangle with him."

ANNOUNCER: In catfish society circles, then, it seems that the
nose is important in recognizing one another. By
picking up chemical messages given off by other

fish, catfish carry on a type of social communication. One chemical signal says this fish is bigger and might cause trouble; another signal may indicate that the fish is nothing to worry about.

Apparently, then, humans are alone in their elaborate attempts to repress body odors. As a matter of fact, the ability of dogs to withstand their owners' perfumed and deodorized bodies remains a wonder, since some scientists have estimated that the dog's sense of smell may be up to 1,000,000 times as keen as that of humans. In *The Hidden Dimension,* anthropologist Edward T. Hall takes this view: "In the use of the olfactory [sense of smell] apparatus Americans are culturally underdeveloped. The extensive use of deodorants and the suppression of odor in public places results in a land of olfactory blandness and sameness that would be difficult to duplicate anywhere else in the world. This blandness . . . deprives us of richness and variety in our life."

Thus, most animals rely heavily on their ability to decipher chemical messages, a skill relatively poorly developed in humans. Again, Dr. Atema:

Even humans with their very sophisticated ways of communication still use chemical communication, in a variety of ways. And one that is becoming more popular, but is in certain countries, like here, still very unpopular, is the one that is currently called "body odor," and I'm convinced that it is in some cases a very important mode of communication. And the reason it doesn't speak so much to us, or the reason we think it is not that important, is because the information is repressed not only socially, but also very effectively by deodorants. But, there is another aspect to that, because it is—or I should say probably because it is—such an ancient way of communication, it arrives at a station in the brain where it is subconscious and not conscious. So it may exert a very profound influence on us—setting our mood, which it usually does, and we will still not be aware of it.

Humans, then, are capable of consciously directing only so much communication and no more. Much of the process is unconscious.

Sound, like odor, plays a critical role in nonhuman communication. The shrill, chirping summer sound of the katydid or cricket may indicate calling, courtship, aggression, or alarm. Cicadas, for instance, use sound to direct the members of the species to a particular tree. Grasshoppers, too, use the same method to gather the group in one place. The male cricket will literally "change his tune" if another male wanders into his territory, lashing out with his antennae, even biting, until one or the other gives up and retreats. And in tropical regions of Africa, there are families of birds which sing duets. This "duetting," according to ethologist E. H. Thorpe, is performed with precise coordination with two birds singing at the same time, "each coordinating its individual song pattern with the other." Thorpe, who has studied these singing birds since 1962, explains in *Scientific American* (August 1973) that so exacting are the songs that they can be "almost completely specified by the pitch of the notes, by the intervals (the difference in pitch between any two notes), by whether the sounds come in harmonic intervals (simultaneously) or in melodic intervals (successively) and by the duration of the notes, their timing and their overall pattern." The vocal sounds of canines—growling, barking, whining—are not, Dr. Michael Fox tells us, "messages akin to words," but can act as signals and, therefore, have "message value." In *Understanding Your Dog*, Fox explains that a "dog's growl and bark warn his owner of an intruder, and a bark by a female wolf will send her cubs running for cover."

In "The Mysterious Language of the Sea," Dr. Todd of Woods Hole indicates that the social organization of whales is the pinnacle of sea life and is based on "a wide range of vocal signals. . . ." He focuses at one point on the song of the humpback whale:

> It usually lasts for about forty-five minutes but in some instances an hour or more depending on the individual who is singing. It is repeated almost identically, time and time again. [The low-frequency sounds pulsate outwards for hundreds and possibly even thousands of miles if unobstructed.]
>
> . . . marine behaviorists suspect that the lower frequency sounds indicate the species and perhaps provide clues to the location of the singer, thus enabling whales to find each other over wide stretches of the ocean.

We'll look more closely at the communication possibilities presented by the vocal sounds of the humpback whale shortly.

Fireflies, finally, pose a particularly interesting study in communication: most adult fireflies flash their lights after dark to attract the opposite sex in order to mate. The renowned entomologist Howard Ensign Evans explains that in "any given locality, the males and females are highly attuned to one another's messages, that is, the variation in responsiveness is such that they almost never answer another species." He calls this flashing of the light organs "a unique means of communication."

So, while the structure of a firefly's light organs themselves can be termed complex, and its means of communication unique, there is nothing in the communication process of any species of firefly—or ant

The flash patterns of males of six species of the genus Photinus.
Each is signaling to the female of his own species in his own characteristic pattern. No. 1 flies two to four yards high and produces three
slow flashes in series. No. 2 flies in a rather straight path somewhat
lower, producing single flashes that increase in intensity during
emission. No. 3 is a low flier that emits a long flash while executing
a lateral curve, while no. 4 makes a series of hops between which
he hovers and produces a quick flash. No. 5 is Photinus pyralis with
its characteristic J-shaped signal. No. 6 is a low-flying species which
produces a long flash while jerking rapidly from side to side. (Courtesy Daniel Otte, James Lloyd, and the Museum of Zoology, University of Michigan.)

or dog or catfish, for that matter—that is comparable to the use of an
extensive vocal and written symbolic process.

One possible exception brings us back to the singing humpback
whale, whose extensive variety of melodic sounds, called songs, forms
what underwater expert Jacques Cousteau calls an "impressive repertoire." As he makes clear, we do not yet know how to decode this language—if it can be called such—but the whale's higher notes do
vary, possibly reflecting the "immediate mood of the singer."

During the filming of ABC-TV's "The Humpback Whale," Cousteau discussed the communication capabilities of the whale (from a
human's point of view) with William C. Cummings, head of Applied Biocoustics at the Naval Undersea Center in San Diego. During the discussion Cummings made the point that while there is no

experimental evidence relating a particular sound of the humpback whale to any specific behavior, we do know that it is unlikely that this remarkable creature would have evolved such a complex mechanism and repertoire of sounds unless they carried information. He agreed with Cousteau that the energy and metric quality of the whale songs are as beautiful and melodious as those of birds and humans.

Cummings made the additional point that no human voice could measure up to the power of the whale's song, an extraordinary melody lasting from nine to eighteen minutes in length and then repeated at long intervals. The human voice is also incapable of reaching its extremely low pitch. It is at least possible that these songs are symbolically meaningful as well as beautiful.

The communication capabilities of the dolphin have been studied more extensively, and more details of its workings are known. In *The Mind of the Dolphin*, John Cunningham Lilly makes clear that dolphins do not just repeat the same sounds monotonously:

> Only if the dolphins are badly and continuously frightened are the sounds emitted monotonous and repetitious. When a dolphin wishes to talk about an object at a distance with another dolphin and wishes to describe how that object moved and at what velocities, he can do it merely by transmitting the proper frequency pattern in his clicks and whistles.
>
> We have demonstrated that the dolphin can do certain vocal tasks that no other animal except man can do. No parrot, no mynah bird, no monkey can do these tasks at all.

Human babies have a drive to copy the sounds they hear other humans making around them (the process of mimicry); the bottlenose dolphin has a similar ability to mimic sounds which occur in its environment. "In the case of the parrot and of the mynah bird," says Lilly, "the mimicry does not seem to be an attempt to communicate. In the case of the human child, the mimicry is such an attempt . . . The parrot and the mynah bird use their vocalization apparatus with a certain degree of success in playing back only limited numbers of words."

In an experiment conducted at the Dolphin Point Laboratory of the Communication Research Institute, St. Thomas, United States Virgin Islands, Margaret Howe lived with a dolphin named Peter for two and a half months in 1965. Her account of learning to communicate with Peter describes the dolphin's ability to vary its vocal ranges. During the second week, Margaret Howe was able to report, "I count, 'one, two, three,' my voice will often rise on 'three' . . . and often Peter will copy this rise in the last of the three sounds."

Though the experiments could not demonstrate that dolphins understand the meanings we attach to our sounds, Margaret Howe could report after the two and a half month experiment that Peter would initiate conversations, "speaking and listening, at any time of day or night. . . . Peter himself will often call to me or start to speak when I am with him. . . ."

In what was perhaps the most revealing incident, Howe reported that Peter "has been practicing with the pronunciation of the letter 'M' from Margaret . . . and is discovering that rolling slightly so that his blowhole is just under the water gives a satisfactory 'M' effect."

This sophistication is not present in the communications system of the firefly, which we could hardly expect to vary the pattern of its flash signals; or in the ant, which must rely on the limited selection of odors it emits. Similar unvarying patterns are found to a greater or lesser extent in the other animal groups we have mentioned. Confusion is kept to a minimum in communication among insects and most other nonhumans.

Even the closest evolutionary relatives of humans, the chimpanzees, with their ability to communicate in very sophisticated ways, cannot vary speech patterns and writing patterns in the manner of humans, nor in the manner of dolphins.

One chimpanzee, named Washoe, was trained by two American scientists to use the American sign language used by the deaf, and another, named Sarah, was trained by psychiatrist David Premack to use different colored chips to designate different types of fruits. Sarah's use of this nonverbal language led Premack to his belief that Sarah understands human language. He warns cynics that Sarah "understands well enough to teach her teachers."

> During a preposition test one day, Sarah, who became restless, gave Mary [Sarah's trainer] what amounted to a sentence-completion test. Sarah put up a partial statement on one side of the language board (A is on . . .) and then arranged alternate answers on the other side. Sarah would point to each possible answer, and Mary's task (which took her a good while to figure out) was to nod when Sarah pointed to the right one. "The little devil would pass by the solution quickly and try to trick me into a mistake," Mary reported.

. . . the chimpanzee has not developed the power of speech.
—*Jane Goodall*

Still, Professor Premack admits the history of failures in teaching monkeys and apes to talk and reports himself that "speech appears to be anatomically impossible for them."

And Jane van Lawick-Goodall, who for a decade studied chimpanzees in the wild in Tanzania, Africa, has found "striking similarities" between humans and chimpanzees in postural and gestural communication signals: "the cheering pat, the embrace of exuberance, the clasp of hands." But, says Goodall, even "the most intensive efforts to teach young chimps to talk have met with virtually no success. Verbal language represents a truly gigantic stride forward in human evolution." Thus, despite their wide range of calls—which do convey basic information—these calls "cannot for the most part be compared to a spoken language," because they are signals, not symbols.

Humans use both signs and symbols to communicate. So far as researchers have been able to prove, all other animals operate on the sign level only, totally incapable of the variation required to manipulate and master the vocal use of symbols.

Our intricate process of communication made through the extensive use of symbols, vocal and written, is ours alone—our blessing and our curse.

SIGNS AND SYMBOLS

In their natural state, animals respond in an amazingly consistent manner so that it is possible to observe repeated and virtually identical performances.
—Edward T. Hall

The human communication process, for all its blessings, brings with it the danger of a great deal of confusion. In animals, the instinctive system of signals—whether odors or sounds or flashing lights—allows for little variation in some cases and none whatsoever in others. It is this lack of variation that makes nonhuman systems of communication more accessible than human language to study and experiment. Animal signals are in this way not at all the same as the human symbolic process, which thrives precisely on its ability to change.

To fully appreciate our use of language, it becomes important to distinguish between the elementary nonhuman systems of sign communication and the highly advanced human system of symbolic communication. Humans also can and do react to signs, of course. Some of these signs are human inventions (the ringing of the alarm clock in the morning); others are part of nature (a funnel shaped cloud moving rapidly across the countryside).

Thirty years ago Suzanne Langer, a philosopher, teacher, and writer, distinguished signs from symbols in this way: "In every case," she wrote, "a sign is closely bound up with something to be noted or expected in experience. It is always a part of the situation to which it refers . . ." Signs, for the most part, provoke in humans what they provoke in nonhumans—a reaction, some kind of response, usually imminent if not immediate. For example, the female firefly an-

A sign is always imbedded in reality . . . but a symbol may be divorced from reality altogether.
—*Suzanne Langer*

swers the male's signal flash, with neither one entertaining the slightest notion of changing that flash pattern to find out if other species are indeed "having more fun." And we humans, while driving our cars, respond to flashing lights with about the same degree of variation: we stop on red and on green. Our actions are closely tied to the signs we are given, and we are given many of them during the course of a day.

On the other hand, a symbol, Langer went on to say, "differs from a sign in that it does not announce the presence of the object, but merely brings the thing to mind." Thus, signs elicit a particular reaction; symbols—varied as they are and removed from reality—elicit something much more: contemplation. And humans alone are capable of this symbolic process which brings such contemplation into play.

This distinction between signs and symbols is not an easy concept to grasp; it takes some mulling over and working out. The discussion and examples that follow will help to make the differences clear.

If someone showed you this sculpture and asked you what it is, you would undoubtedly say that it is a horse. You wouldn't mean, of course, that it was a "real" horse, not one that you would at-

Courtesy, Fogg Art Museum, Harvard University. Bequest of Mrs. John Nicholas Brown

Prancing Horse, T'ang Dynasty

tempt to saddle and ride, three dimensional though it is. Without thinking consciously about it, you would realize that it is in fact merely a representation of a horse, an arrangement of shapes, lines and curves that remind you of a horse. What you see here, then, is a symbol of a horse, a fourteen-and-one-half-inch-high statue that brings a prancing horse to mind. (In fact, what you see here is a picture of a statue.)

In this same way, you could if you wanted stand all day in front of Edouard Manet's painting *Races at Longchamp* without the least fear of being trampled by the horses bearing down on the very spot where you are standing. And though the horses in this painting look a good deal more like horses you have seen roaming fields or have ridden than does the T'ang Dynasty statuette, still you know that what you are looking at is symbolic, that there is no danger whatever in not moving aside. The horses, the people, even the racetrack itself, are mere representations, symbols, which bring to mind all the things included in the picture—and possibly many things that are not. This is the symbolic process at work.

Courtesy of The Art Institute of Chicago. Potter Palmer Collection.

The Races at Longchamp, Paris, Eduoard Manet, 1864

The following cartoon is also a representation. We could, after all, wait and wait for the horses to stride forward, take a great leap over the hedgerow, and land amid the coldcuts, pickles, and beer. It will never happen, not if we wait forever.

Drawing by Alain; © 1936, 1964 The New Yorker Magazine, Inc.

. . . signs refer to actual situations, in which things have obvious relations to each other that require only to be noted, but symbols refer to ideas, which are not physically there for inspection, so their connections and features have to be represented.
—*Suzanne Langer*

But our purpose right now is to make a distinction between signs and symbols, so for the moment suppose that what you see is no cartoon, no mere representation at all, but an actual situation in which the father—supposing himself and his family to be in complete safety, miles from danger—suddenly hears the thundering of horses' hooves bearing down on them from behind. The sound he hears, then, becomes a sign, a warning sign in this case, that we hope will lead to a mad scramble to safety. Nothing less than an immediate reaction is going to save the family from disaster. Such a reaction would be to a sign rather than a symbol.

Reactions to signs, then—even by humans—are different (far less complicated) from reactions to symbols, and nonhumans operate strictly on the sign level. Human communication, on the other hand, is deeply rooted in the far more sophisticated, contemplative symbolic process, with humans themselves reacting only incidentally to sign-level communication as it occurs in their everyday lives.

COMMUNICATION AMONG HUMANS—
THE SYMBOL AT THE CENTER

The use of symbols, "the trait that sets human mentality apart," has been confusing us for a long, long time. We begin, we think, by acquiring language (first spoken, then written) only to find out that it has too often acquired us. We seem adrift in our efforts to communicate with others, and while we realize that no language, no system of communication has the capacity to say all there is to say about everything—or all we mean to say about anything—we remain adrift. We don't understand the symbolic process, this elusive key to our language, and are left feeling separate, apart, even antagonistic. However accurate Hayakawa's description is of language as the "indispensable mechanism," he is no more accurate than Rollo May, who claims that "communication . . . is all but destroyed."

But these are not new problems, just old problems made more intense by the crush of a modern society in which the human desire and need to make contact has become increasingly strong. Language

Bronze, 8½ x 25⅜ x 17¼". Collection, The Museum of Modern Art, New York.

City Square (La Place), Alberto Giacometti, 1948

remains the key to that contact, just as the use of symbols remains the key to language. In other words, communication depends on language, and language depends on symbols. We must concentrate on the symbol in an effort to better understand all the misunderstanding.

For humans there never has been a time when symbols did not have meaningful impact. Apparently even before humans developed their "organized sound language," these symbols took the form of pictures stained on the walls of caves, the most sophisticated of which date from the Later Old Stone Age, sometime between 15,000 and 8,000 B.C. These representations, almost exclusively of animals, worked their way right through the Middle Stone Age, sometime between 8,000 B.C. and 3,000 B.C. (with its marked increase in the number of images of people); to the New Stone Age, dating from 3,000 B.C., at which time humans took a great leap forward by becoming agricultural—what H. W. Janson has called the hunting-to-husbandry revolution.

Courtesy, Archives Photographiques Paris

Bison with Superimposed Arrows

Let's take a closer look at these cave walls. There are two theories about this early picture making. The first maintains that people believed that the actual killing of the beast is made easier by wounding the animal's image. As the bison's image becomes equal in the image maker's mind to the bison itself, its fate is practically sealed; it is virtually commanded to die the moment the painted arrows are superimposed on the animal's painted body. Power of this kind would bring welcome relief to the hungry family of any hunter. As Albert Elsen, an eminent art historian, has pointed out in *Purposes of Art,* "art performed the vital function of assisting men to control their environment whether human or natural, and to intervene in the course of events."

A second theory—comparable to the first in that both assume that symbols "stand for" reality—centers on the possibility of increasing a scarce herd of bison, horses, reindeer, or bulls. To create an abundant herd in pictures was to have an abundant herd in real life. Prehistoric art, as Elsen says, "was seriously involved with life and death, closely interwoven with all phases of human existence," a claim borne out by the Venus of Willendorf. Also dated between 15,000 and 10,000 B.C., and found in Lower Austria, the Venus shows clear evidence of attempts to create an abundance of human life.

Stone, 4⅜" high (cast of original). Natur-historisches Museum, Vienna. Photo, courtesy The American Museum of Natural History, New York.

Venus of Willendorf, c. 15,000–10,000 B.C.

Miles away and centuries removed, the African *akua ba* doll,* carried by expectant mothers, is believed so closely related to the thing it represents that it gives the mother some control over the destiny of her and her child. The doll is designed to lend fertility

* Frank Willett, in *African Art,* says that though some claim that the dolls are directly connected to the *Ankh,* the symbol of life for the much older Egyptian culture, none are, in fact, "likely to be older than the nineteenth century."

Courtesy, Sue Bentley Jackson

Akua ba doll

to the mother and beauty to the unborn infant. The hope of the mother is that the beauty of the doll she carries inside her womb will resemble the idealized beauty of the *akua ba* she carries outside. The "manna (the driving force of all existence)" as Margaret Trowell describes it in *African and Oceanic Art*, was thus "enticed, placated, and harassed for the well being of all."

And what of our own culture? It is certainly not without its symbols, nor without its desires for an "agent of control." How effective these symbols are, how strongly one believes in their power, remains a matter of individual conscience. This is as it should be. That there exists an unshakable belief in the inherent connection between symbols and their referents in human cultures, and that this belief carries over into attitudes about language, is beyond question. The point is that language—whether spoken, written, or silent—involves symbols of a different kind. Language is not a matter of individual conscience, and the inaccuracy and inadequacy of our attempts to communicate with each other are truly disturbing. Rollo May discussed one of the works of a modern French playwright, Eugene Ionesco:

Ionesco has a scene in his play, *The Bald Soprano*, in which a man and woman happen to meet and engage in polite, if mannered, conversation. As they talk they discover that they both came down to [the city] on the ten o'clock train that morning and, surprisingly, the address of both is the same building. . . . Lo and behold, they also both live in the same apartment and both have a daughter seven years old. They finally discover to their astonishment that they are man and wife.

The overriding concern for us is that the encounter dramatized here is being repeated on many levels. Not just on the mass transit systems of major cities, but out in the streets and in the homes of our smallest towns. Language is not the sole culprit; we are just now beginning to understand and tackle the psychological and sociological factors involved. But without a more accurate use of language, discussing these problems in human communication—much less solving them —seems remote indeed. Prehistoric humans had their system of communication and their problems; we have ours. How well they did with their system and with their problems we don't really know; how poorly we are doing with ours seems obvious. Eugene Ionesco is not alone in his perception, nor is Albert Giacometti. There are many others and it might be well that before we take a look at how language works, we think about what has already been said and take notice of how some people look at themselves, at us, and our modern society.

Suggestions

◄§ Take another look at the quote of Mason Williams that appears in the Preface. Can you define awareness?

◄§ Joseph Haydn composed over a hundred symphonies during the eighteenth century, of which one of the better known is the so-called Farewell Symphony. Haydn wrote it in 1772 after having contracted himself in 1761 to his patron, the powerful Hungarian noble Esterhazy family. Haydn's friend and biographer, G. A. Griesinger, relates the circumstances (as told to him by Haydn himself) of the symphony's composition in this way:

> In Prince Esterhazy's orchestra were several vigorous young married men who in summer, when the Prince stayed at Esterhaza castle, had to leave their wives behind in Eistenstadt. Contrary to his custom, the Prince once wished to extend his stay in Esterhaza by several weeks. The fond husbands, especially dismayed at this news turned to Haydn and pleaded with him to do something. Haydn had the notion of writing a symphony which was performed at the first opportunity and each of the musicians was directed, as soon as his part was finished, to put out his candle, pack up his music and, with his instrument under his arm to go away. The Prince and the audience understood the meaning . . . at once, and the next day came the order to depart from Esterhaza.

How does Haydn get his message across; that is, what "language" does he use? Recount any situation from your own experience in which you used a similar method to make your point. How successful were you? Create an imaginary situation in which silence becomes the most effective means of communication.

◄§ The author John C. Condon has made the following distinction between signs and symbols: "A sign stands in a one-to-one relationship with an experience (or object, or the like); a symbol suggests many possible responses." Do you think smoke is a sign or symbol? Explain your answer. A wedding ring? (Consider here whether or not a person is less married if he or she does not wear one.) What about the American flag? What about a yawn? What about steam rising from a bowl of soup? Explain your answers. Name some signs that humans react to. Explain why each is a sign and not a symbol. Name some symbols in our culture, explaining why they are not signs. Tell what the usual emotional response to the symbol is.

◄§ Is the situation in Ionesco's play *The Bald Soprano* realistic; do you think it could really happen? Explain your answer. There is a basic assumption in this chapter that ours is an "alienated" society. Do you agree or disagree? Why?

◄§ Does Giacometti's sculpture appear to you to be an accurate portrayal of the human condition today? Is it in any way related to the scene in Ionesco's play? In *Art Through the Ages,* the authors say of Giacometti's piece that "The pencil-thin, elongated figures striding abstractly through endless space never meet and never can." What is your reaction to this statement? Do you agree or disagree with it? Why or why not?

◄§ On the following pages are works by the contemporary artists George Segal, Jasper Johns, Andy Warhol, and Tom Wesselmann. The art historian Sam Hunter has stated that "the pop artists have taken their imagery directly from the billboards, the supermarkets, and the comic strips, road signs, television, movies and other popular sources." Take a close look at the creations as separate comments and as a total statement on our society. In general, what are they saying? What symbols are they using to say it? How do they create and manipulate their symbols to make their statement? In answering these questions, pay particular attention to the directions, comments, and questions that appear below each work of art.

◄§ Study carefully the sculpture by Segal and read the statement by Hunter. What contact are the people in the sculpture having with one another? How would you describe the looks on their faces? Do they look capable of communicating with one another or are they communicating right now in sending messages about their unwillingness to become involved with each other? If you were in a similar situation, would you attempt to communicate? If so, how?

The dehumanizing impact of our surroundings and the acute sense of alienation [are] at the heart of George Segal's environmental sculptures.
—Sam Hunter

Plaster, metal, and leather, 7 x 4 x 9'. Courtesy, Hirshhorn Museum and Sculpture Garden, Smithsonian Institution.

Bus Riders, George Segal, 1963

◄§   Concentrate on one of the figures. What do you imagine his thoughts and feelings are like? What do you imagine his life is like? Write a brief biographical sketch of him. Write a brief biographical sketch of yourself. What differences exist between you and him? Your life and his?

◄§   Look at Jasper John's *Painted Bronze* and read the accompanying statement. Do you agree that it is by our manufactured products that we are known and will be remembered in the future? If the statement is true, is this necessarily a bad thing? Why or why not? If the statement is true, what comparable items could you place alongside the cans of ale? If you think the statement is true but dislike the thought of it, what can you think of that we would better be remembered by? How do those things symbolize the values of our society?

. . . The flimsy and disposable container, intended to be used and forgotten, is monumentalized and made permanent as a profoundly symbolic twentieth-century artifact. By our manufactured products we are and will be known!
—*Horst de la'Croix & Richard G. Tansey*

5½ x 8 x 4½". Collection of the artist. Photo, Leo Castelli Gallery, New York.

Painted Bronze, Jasper Johns, 1964

◄§   Look at Andy Warhol's *One Hundred Campbell's Soup Cans* and his statement. Do you agree with Warhol's statement? If so, in what ways is the statement true? Do you see everyone's looking alike and acting alike as a good thing? Why or why not? Does it help or hinder communication? In what ways?

◄§   Study Tom Wesselmann's "Great American Still Life." What is a "still life"? What makes this still life different, that is what is the significance of the items Wesselmann has chosen? Do you agree with G. H. Hamilton that this serves as a paradigm (a model) of suburban America?

Everybody
looks alike and
acts alike, and
we're getting
more and more
that way.
—*Andy Warhol*

72 x 52", Kraushar Collection. Photo, Leo Castelli Gallery, New York.

One Hundred Soup Cans, Andy Warhol, 1962

Why only "suburban" conformities? What items would you select from your own background to serve as a model? Make up your own still life that communicates your particular background to the rest of the class.

~§   Read the statements on pages 28–30 by Arthur Jackson and "V.B." Look carefully at David Alfaro Siqueiros' *Echo of a Scream* on page 29.

For your journal:
    What does Arthur Jackson mean when he says that he "never wanted out"? What is it he wanted "in" to? If you ever felt as he does, explain

4 x 5′. Private collection, West Germany.

Great American Still Life #19, Tom Wesselmann, 1962

the circumstances. What two basic questions does V.B. ask? Have you ever asked yourself the same questions? What answers does V.B. arrive at? What answers have you arrived at? Do you agree that in order to survive, a person must not think such thoughts? How does your reaction to these questions change if you know that these are teenage "voices from the ghetto," ages 15 and 14 respectively?

Though Siqueiros' painting was inspired by the brutality of the Spanish Civil War, it is a plea for humans to avoid all wars. How, then, does this painting which focuses on victims bear upon the statements? That is, is there any way in which Arthur Jackson and V.B. are "victims" and "at war"?

*I have felt lonely, forgotten or even left
out, set apart from the rest of the world.
I never wanted out. If anything, I wanted
in.*

—Arthur Jackson

*For what purpose was I born? I don't see.
To speak words that no one will listen to
No matter how loud I shout them?
To throw up dates, and events*

Duco on wood, 48 x 36". Collection, The Museum of Modern Art, New York. Gift of Edward M. M. Warburg.

Echo of a Scream, David Alfaro Siqueiros, 1937

*just as I recorded them and be pronounced
a genius? To sit through school day after
day and be referred to as a "good child"?
To hear things that I shouldn't and then be
instructed to forget?*

*For what reason am I living? To see
men destroy each other, and we listen
to them preach godlyness and good-will?*

To take things as they are and never question?
To live a clean life, only to rot away in your
grave? To have things your soul desires, prohibited?
To be told God is good, but disregard the fact
that the world—his so called "creation"
is bad?

But these are thoughts I must
not think if I am to survive.

—*V.B.*

◄§ Read the words to the two songs, and look at the preceding picture.

For your journal:

How would you compare these songs? Does the first accurately reflect an existing world as opposed to the second, which we can only
"imagine"? If so, in what ways? Does the first accurately portray everyone at least to some degree? Does it portray you? If so, in what ways?
Does Andrew Wyeth's painting *Christina's World* have anything to do
with the song, "Eleanor Rigby"? Explain your answer. Does the second
seem ideal? For everyone? For you? What would a world without countries be like? Without religions? Without possessions? How would you
imagine an ideal world? Pick a song that you think depicts a certain mood.
Bring the words of the song to class and discuss it.

Tempera on gesso panel, 32¼ x 47¾". Collection, The Museum of Modern Art, New
York. Purchase.

Christina's World, Andrew Wyeth, 1948

◄§ From your own experience, what can you add *to your journal* about communication among nonhumans, signs and symbols, the symbolic system, or the arbitrary nature of language?

Eleanor Rigby

Ah, look at all the lonely people!
Ah, look at all the lonely people!

Eleanor Rigby
Picks up the rice in the church where a wedding has been
Lives in a dream
Waits at the window
Wearing the face that she keeps in a jar by the door.
Who is it for?

All the lonely people,
Where do they all come from?
All the lonely people,
Where do they all belong?

Father McKenzie,
Writing the words of a sermon that no one will hear,
No one comes near
Look at him working,
Darning his socks in the night when there's nobody there
What does he care?

All the lonely people,
Where do they all come from?
All the lonely people,
Where do they all belong?

Ah, look at all the lonely people!
Ah, look at all the lonely people!

Eleanor Rigby
Died in the church and was buried along with her name
Nobody came
Father McKenzie,
Wiping the dirt from his hands as he walks from the grave,
No one was saved.

All the lonely people,
Where do they all come from?
All the lonely people,
Where do they all belong?

Ah, look at all the lonely people!
Ah, look at all the lonely people!

—John Lennon and Paul McCartney

Imagine

imagine there's no heaven
it's easy if you try
no hell below us
above us only sky
imagine all the people
living for today . . .

imagine there's no countries
it isn't hard to do
nothing to kill or die for
and no religion too
imagine all the people
living life in peace . . .

imagine no possessions
i wonder if you can
no need for greed or hunger a brotherhood of man
imagine all the people
sharing all the world . . .

you may say i'm a dreamer
but i'm not the only one
i hope someday you'll join us
and the world will be as one

—John Lennon

2 How Language Works

THE SYMBOLIC SYSTEM

Suppose I sent you the following message:

$$-\square\lceil\nabla\odot\setminus- \quad \cap\otimes^{\square} \quad \cap\otimes\nabla\vdash\rangle\otimes\cap\otimes\square$$

It wouldn't mean very much to you unless the two of us had worked out some previous agreement as to what each of the strange looking shapes means. If we had worked out a systematic relationship between the different shapes above and the shapes that appear everywhere else on the page, I think you would be willing to accept the fact that we could work out our own system of written communication. If, for example, everytime I use the shape " $\cap$ " to match what we know as the letter A, we would have a start to our own alphabet.

This arrangement shouldn't strike you as being so strange if you remember that you did the same thing in grade school. You agreed that certain lines and curves stood for certain sounds, which in turn stood for certain things in the world around you. The teacher and all your classmates agreed with you. So before entering school you had learned to talk. You used words that fit an implicit agreement with those around you. You didn't realize you were using a conventional symbolic system, and when you entered school you began to learn still another symbolic system, which also would soon become habitual, writing.

At that time, that is when you first began to write, do you think it would have been any more difficult to learn, for instance, that the shape ∇ stood for (was a symbol of) the initial sound we make when we say the word "boy"? Think about it. Is there some inherent relationship between "b" as it is written and the sound we make each time we say it? If you had learned in grade school that ∇

33

was the symbol for what we actually use as the second letter of our alphabet, would it look so strange to you now?

Is there something more logical about $| + \supset = b$ than $| + - + / = \triangledown$ in the sound that begins the word "begin"? It boils down to this:

$$| + \supset = b \qquad | + - + / = \triangledown$$

$b = \triangledown$, the written symbol for the initial sound of "boy."

Are the shapes *b* and *o* and *y* the only ones we could have learned to place side by side in a certain order to arrive at the written equivalent of the sound we make when we say the word *boy*? We failed then to see the distinction between the shapes of letters and the sounds we made and carried this failure right on through to another assumption: that words are somehow necessarily—even magically—related to the things they merely stand for.

Take the word *chair*, an auditory symbol of the chair a person sits down in. The letters we learn to write, c-h-a-i-r, are symbols (written) of a symbol (the word we speak out loud) of something we can touch and see and use everyday. In this same way, all written words are symbols of symbols; but, again, no magical connection is at work, only the natural human desire to want to be in control of what happens to us. This is an instinct we share with the makers of cave paintings and *akua ba* dolls.

Suggestions

  By matching these new symbols I have created with those you are very familiar with, decipher the message at the beginning of this chapter.

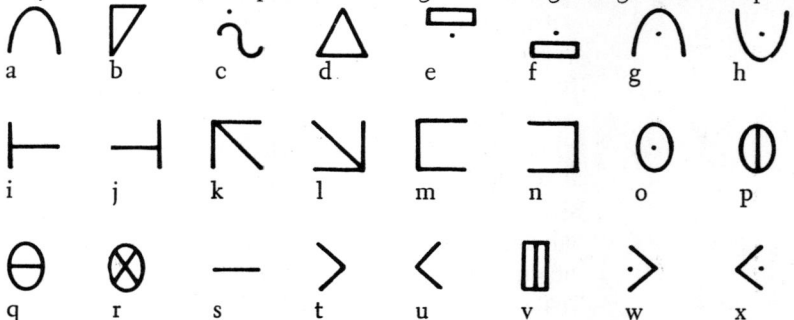

a   b   c   d   e   f   g   h

i   j   k   l   m   n   o   p

q   r   s   t   u   v   w   x

y   z

◆§ Give your own definition of the word *arbitrary*. Explain the sentence, "Letters are arbitrary symbols for the sounds of our language." Discuss it in terms of the deciphered statement. Explain how it applies to language.

◆§ Decode the following message:

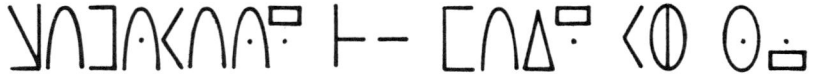

[coded symbol message]

◆§ Define the word *system,* in the sentence "The system isn't operating smoothly." What is a system? Describe a system that you are familiar with. How does it operate? What does language have in common with other systems that you are familiar with? How, then, is language a system?

SYMBOLS ARE ARBITRARY

Symbols, then, sounded or written, are arbitrary. Language, being made up of symbols is likewise arbitrary. This arbitrary system becomes a method, a vehicle, used to get something from one place to another—in this case, a thought or feeling from somewhere inside your mind into someone else's.

What gives a significance to language is meaningful transfer.
—*Mario Pei*

Some of these messages are easier to send than others, usually depending on how tangible the items are that we're talking about. A message about a car or crocodile is easier to send (and receive) in spoken language than a message about love or hate. Still, sending the easiest of messages accurately and having it received accurately is at best a shaky proposition. In fact, it is often those times when we're most sure the message is clear that we find out later the message has been most misunderstood. It happens to all of us. What we think we have said accurately is misconstrued by our listeners. What we say is not at all what we meant. This all goes on within the most sophisticated means of communication known to humans—their language.

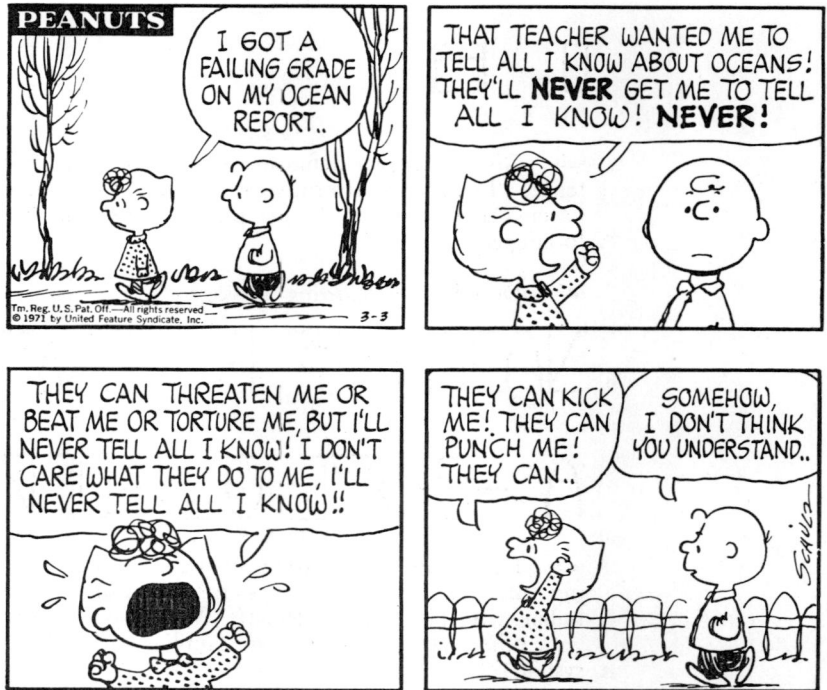

Language—these arbitrary systems of symbols, written and spoken —could have come down to us through time looking and sounding very different from what it does now. Wouldn't we have adopted without question the shapes that appear under "Greek" in the table shown here? Isn't the fact that the lines and shapes changed an indication that further change will occur? At the same time we have also adopted without question the combination of sounds that make up our spoken language. Some of these combinations, symbolized (represented) by combinations of letters, are common in the English language; some are not. Language expert Stuart Chase gives an example: "An advertising man in his cubicle on Madison Avenue, after a week of dreaming, may christen a new breakfast food 'crunchy, vitamin-packed THRUB,' but he cannot call it DLUB, not in English he can't. If he tried to name it NFPK, a common sound in other tongues, he would undoubtedly be fired . . . English permits no words to begin with NG, but Eskimo is full of them." In addition, says Chase, "MPST . . . can be pronounced as in 'glimpsed'; KSTHS, as in 'sixth.' On the other hand, the formula for English speakers rejects sound combinations readily pronounceable in other languages, such as LITK, FPAT, NWENG, DZOGB."

NORTH SEMITIC				GREEK				ETRUSCAN		LATIN			MODERN CAPS		
EARLY	EARLY HEBREW	MOABITE	PHOEN.	EARLY	EAST.	WEST.	CLASS.	EARLY	CLASS.	EARLY	MONUM	CLASS.	BLACK LETTER	ITALIC	ROMAN

(Table of the evolution of alphabetic letterforms from North Semitic through Greek, Etruscan, Latin, to Modern Caps, showing each letter A through Z and additional Greek signs.)

From *Writing* by David Diringer. Copyright © David Diringer 1962. Reprinted by permission of Praeger Publishers, Inc., New York.

Suggestions

◆§ Divide the class into groups of three, and have each person create nine new symbols (the alphabet's twenty-seventh symbol can be used as an end mark of punctuation—a period, question mark, and so on.) Each person must get the other two to agree to his or her share of the newly created shapes. It will be easier if there is agreement within the group that the new symbols will correspond to the letters of the alphabet we ordinarily use. After the group has reached its agreement on all the newly created symbols each member must send a written message using the new alphabet (no fewer than six words) to the person on the left, who must then decipher the message. Check the accuracy of the message you received with the person who sent it.

⋞ Make up two new symbols for "th," one as it is sounded in the words "this" and "that" and the other as it is sounded in the words "theater" and "thirteen."

⋞ Discuss with the rest of the class the perceptions you gained about language from taking part in the exercises.

⋞ Pressure is mounting to switch the United States to the metric system of measurements, linear, liquid, dry, and so on. So it may not be too long before someone asks you how many kilometers it is from St. Louis to Denver. Explain how more than just mathematics will be involved in giving that person an accurate answer. Is inconvenience the only reason some people are reluctant to make the change?

LINEAR MEASURE

English Unit	Metric Unit
1 inch =	25.4 millimeters
	2.54 centimeters
1 foot =	30.48 centimeters
	3.048 decimeters
	0.3048 meter
1 yard =	0.9144 meter
1 mile =	1609.3 meters
	1.6093 kilometers
0.03937 inch	= 1 millimeter
0.3937 inch	= 1 centimeter
3.937 inches	= 1 decimeter
39.37 inches	
3.2808 feet	= 1 meter
1.0936 yards	
3280.8 feet	
1093.6 yards	= 1 kilometer
0.62137 mile	

Reprinted by permission from *The Random House Dictionary of the English Language.* Copyright © 1966, 1973 by Random House, Inc.

WORDS DON'T MEAN . . .

I am Dick Gregory; I live in America; I am a Negro. I am an individual first, an American second, and a Negro third. If a man

Words in themselves, then, as they are sounded or written, carry no meaning per se, that is, works do not mean in and of themselves —only people do. For symbols are symbols, mere devices—and we should treat them accordingly. Only through our continued lack of awareness do they continue to control us. When Humpty Dumpty says "When I use a word, it means just what I want it to mean—

calls me a nigger,
he is calling me
something I am
not. The nigger
exists only in his
own mind; there-
fore his mind is
the nigger. I must
feel sorry for such
a man.
—Dick Gregory

neither more nor less," he goes on to explain, "The question is which is to be master—that's all."

Suggestions

◄§   What does Dick Gregory mean when he says "The nigger exists only in his [the other man's] mind"? What does Gregory understand about the use of words and their relationship to reality?

◄§   Try this. On page 40 is a page of sheet music. Pick up your book and place the notes to your ear. Then answer the following questions.

What do you hear? How does this experiment make clearer the distinction between a symbol and the thing it symbolizes? (This is a portion of a famous piece of music, the beginning of the second movement of Beethoven's *Piano Concerto No. 5*, the "Emperor Concerto." You may also have heard it in the melody of "Somewhere" from Leonard Bernstein's *West Side Story*.)

◄§   Take a close look at the 18th century graphic *The Enraged Musician* by William Hogarth on page 41.
     Note the hautboy (oboe) player, the man on horseback blowing a horn, the yelling fish peddler, the cats on the rooftop howling at each other, the girl with a milkpail on her head calling her wares, a pregant woman holding a child in her arms while singing a ballad ("The Ladies Fall") as the parrot above her head echoes her, a boy and girl making their particular noises, another boy beating a drum while playing soldier, and a dog barking at the noisy knife-grinder. Finally, note the flag on the steeple indicating a day of public rejoicing, which means the ringing of church bells.
     Can you explain why the English novelist Fielding claimed that this Hogarth graphic was "enough to make a man deaf to look at it"? Does it "deafen" you? Explain your answer. How is Fielding's statement—and yours—related to the experiment with the sheet music?

◄§   Read the following poem by Richard Brautigan.

   "Star-Spangled" Nails

   You've got
   some "star-spangled"
       nails
   in your coffin, kid.
   That's what
   they've done for you,
       son

Is Brautigan in some way concerned with how symbols are confused with what they stand for? In what ways? What symbols is he referring to?

Courtesy, Ernst Eulenburg, Ltd.

◄§ From everyday situations or conversations, or from anything occur-
ring in the mass media, find examples of situations where a symbol and
the thing it symbolizes are confused with each other. *In your journal*
explain how the confusions arose, and discuss them with the class.

The Enraged Musician, William Hogarth

3 Additional Aspects

LEVELS OF ABSTRACTION AND CLASSIFICATION

Consider the following circumstances:

Mr. A is in the park strolling with his dog and is addressed by Mr. B who happens by. Mr. B nods hello and, noticing the dog, speaks to Mr. A.

MR. B: Ah! That's a beautiful dog you have there. (The dog sniffs Mr. B and its tail begins to wag.) What's his name?

MR. A: (Somewhat indignantly) *He* is a *she*.

MR. B: (Remains pleasant) Oh. Sorry.

MR. A: (Now looking less annoyed) Her name is Brandy.

MR. B: Brandy, huh? (Bends down and runs his hand down the length of Brandy's back) Hi, Brandy. (Looks up at the owner) What kind is she? A bassett hound?

MR. A: (Suddenly scowling) What kind? Do you mean what breed? (He doesn't wait for a reply and answers in a haughty manner.) Brandy is a beagle, sir.

MR. B: Really! Well, I've heard beagles make great pets.

MR. A: (Frowning noticeably) We think of her as a member of the family, not as a pet.

MR. B: (Noticing the noticeable frown) Oh. She's just a puppy, isn't she? (Hoping he finally gets something right)

MR. A: (The frown disappears) Yep. Just a puppy.

MR. B: (A bit relieved but eager to get away) Well, I'll be on my way. (Pats the beagle puppy named Brandy once more, rises, nods to Mr. A, and departs—having liked Brandy more than Mr. A)

The focus of this rather typical conversation finds Mr. B considering the dog Brandy in several different ways. When Mr. A and Brandy come into Mr. B's view and then come close by, Mr. B strikes up a conversation (though not a very successful one) with Mr. A. During the conversation Mr. B refers to Brandy as a "dog" in one instance

. . . the observations we make are incomplete . . .

and as a "pet" in another instance. In trying to determine Brandy's gender, Mr. B is considering her in another way; and when Mr. B tries to determine her breed, he is considering her in still another way. Then, after finding out that Brandy is a beagle, he guesses (correctly, for a change) that she is a puppy.

Brandy, therefore, has, within a few moments, been considered from the standpoint of gender (female), breed (beagle), age (puppy), and status (a member of the family, as opposed to a mere pet). She has been considered as an individual creature ("Her name is Brandy") and as a member of several different groups (females, beagles, puppies, and pets) with which she shares similar characteristics. Nothing unusual. Brandy is, after all, many things simultaneously.

But before detailing this conversation further we need to consider important circumstances that existed when Mr. B first saw Mr. A and Brandy. We are interested particularly in the process of abstraction—what it is and how it works—which began for Mr. B the moment he looked at Mr. A's four-legged, long-tailed, floppy-eared companion. He perceived her as he would perceive anything with his senses, in this case the sense of sight, with the naked eye, and the sense of touch, when he strokes her back with his hand. This is the level of our ordinary daily perceptions known as the *macroscopic* level, which includes, in addition to what is seen by the eyes or touched by the hand, whatever is smelled, heard, or tasted. Thus, the process of abstraction begins for us on this level, since abstraction is

. . . our eyes do not give us a complete picture of an apple or a pencil or a fit of anger . . .

Courtesy, Dennis Berner

Macroscopic level, the level of ordinary perception, whatever is seen by the naked eye or touched by the hand.

. . . observation is the process of abstracting.
—*Wendell Johnson*

a matter of selecting a part of the whole. For we do not see *all* of an object at any given moment.

For instance, how much do we see when we look at something, as, for example, when Mr. B looks at Brandy? When we pick up a pencil, what do we see? Without rolling it in our fingers, do we see *all* of it? Do we have the *capability* of seeing *all* of anything at any one moment? The answer is no. There is always a part we will not see without moving the object itself or without moving around the object. Mr. B sees only a side view, or, at the most, a three-quarter view, of Brandy as she comes into view. This is the process of abstraction, the process of selection, already at work. And remember, conversation has not even begun yet.

The process of abstraction (of selection) of portions of objects occurs since we are not capable of seeing at a given moment all there is to see. We select some parts and disregard others. To abstract means to select, or remove, a part of the total, and this is what happens whenever we look at something.

The macroscopic is only one level on which the process of abstraction operates. It is a continuous process from level to level. For not only has Mr. B seen only part of Brandy on the macroscopic level of his perception, he has seen nothing of her on the *microscopic* level.

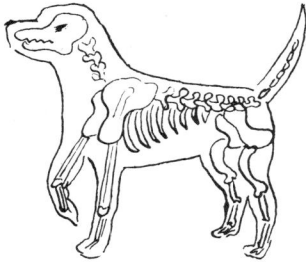

Microscopic level, the level which cannot be seen by the naked eye alone, but can be seen only with the aid of a microscope, x-ray, etc.

Courtesy, Dennis Berner

If we aid our everyday perception with equipment such as a microscope or x-ray machine, we are then able to perceive objects on this microscopic level of bone structure and muscle tissue. On this level, with the proper equipment, we are able to see what we could not possibly see with the naked eye. Mr. B would get a substantially different view of Brandy on this level—an additional view. But it would be the same Brandy nonetheless.

There is still another level on which we must consider Brandy. In addition to the macroscopic and microscopic levels, there is the *submicroscopic*, a level which humans are unable to perceive at all with either their human senses or external equipment. This is the level that science assures us exists, the world of atoms and electrons, constantly rotating, reacting to the environment, changing the makeup of the items themselves—whether a living organism or not, whether a human being, a puppy, or a table top. We accept the word of the scientists on this one, that the submicroscopic level does exist and is a part of everything in the universe.

What happens altogether is this: When we see something—we

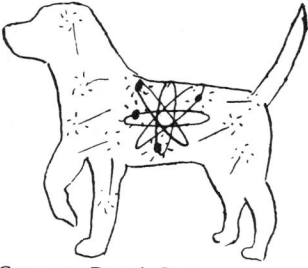

Courtesy, Dennis Berner

Submicroscopic level, which
is below the level of perception, unaided or aided. The
world of electrons and atoms,
which science has assured us
exists.

pick up a book and thumb through it, or see a dog stroll past us—
all three of these levels are operating simultaneously, though we are
capable initially of only the ordinary level of our everyday perceptions, the *macroscopic* level. But, again, what we are able to see in
our everyday experience is not all that is there; we take in only so
much of an object and no more. Put a page of that book under the
microscope or take an x-ray of that strolling dog, and we can see
things we were unable to see with the naked eye—this forms the
microscopic level of perception. And that other level, the *submicroscopic*, is one that humans with their most powerful microscope or
x-ray machine have never seen, a level we cannot perceive no matter
what we carry around with, or attached to, us. Based on their method
of investigation, scientists have inferred (concluded) that this level
does exist and that all material things in the universe (made up as they
are of these constantly swirling electrons and atoms) are constantly
changing. This change is more readily seen in some objects than in
others. A stick of butter left out in mid-August will show its changing
nature more rapidly than the picnic table on which it was left, but
nevertheless the table will also have been changing.

What we have focused on to this point—the macroscopic, microscopic, and submicroscopic levels of existence (of the object itself,
the thing perceived) and levels of perception (by the observer)—are
the nonverbal levels of abstraction, since all that has taken place
up to now has done so without the use of a single word. All things
exist, then, on these three levels simultaneously—without a word
having been spoken or written. Mr. B's macroscopic level of perception is operating normally as he focuses his attention on the pompous
Mr. A and particularly on Mr. A's puppy. In gazing at Mr. A's puppy,
Mr. B has unconsciously dismissed the microscopic and submicroscopic levels of Brandy's total existence. Mr. B is paying no conscious
attention whatever to Brandy's physiological or emotional makeup,
nor to her bone and muscle structure. He cares least of all about the
movement of electrons and atoms as they go about their business
somewhere (everywhere) within the confines of Brandy's skin. He is

conscious about only what he actually sees; what he sees is what he has selected (abstracted) from the total Brandy; he can see nothing of Brandy's unique and separate microscopic and submicroscopic levels of existence.

So much for the nonverbal levels of abstraction. But what happens when we begin to use words? For one thing, the process of abstrac-

Dogs

"Brandy" is now even less an individual than on previous level, because only the characteristics that make her resemble other dogs are considered.

Courtesy, Dennis Berner

tion continues. It travels through all levels, nonverbal and verbal alike. The moment Mr. B refers to what he sees as a *dog* he has selected only the features that Brandy has in common with other

"Brandy"

"Brandy," apart from every other creature or object in the universe. This is the first verbal level. The individual creature has been named.

Courtesy, Dennis Berner

similar creatures. That is, he has selected from Brandy only what his previous experience with other creatures with four legs, a tail, and the like, has taught him are called *dogs*. Brandy herself is, after all, a unique creature with a name of her own, to say nothing of a personality of her own, to say nothing of the fact that no other creature is exactly like her in every respect—or even precisely like her in *any* respect. Mr. B, then, in using the term *dog*, has dismissed much about this single creature, not even having acknowledged that she is a particular breed. This is the selection or abstraction process at work. In using the word *dog*, Mr. B placed himself on a higher level of abstraction (having dismissed more characteristics—thereby selecting less—about Brandy as an individual) than he would have had he known more about dogs in general and beagles and Brandy in particular. Had he considered *beagles*, he would have been more specific than

Beagles

Courtesy, Dennis Berner

"Brandy" is suddenly grouped with other beagles, thereby losing some of her individuality as she is now considered more as a type (beagle) than as herself (Brandy).

when he considered *dogs;* still, he would not have been thinking of Brandy as an individual but only as part of a group whose members resemble one another closely enough to be given a general name—in this case the name *beagles*.

So the various aspects (or levels) from which Mr. B views Brandy —as a *dog, female, breed, pet,* and *puppy*—are ways of grouping her with others, and this process of grouping is known as classification. Classification continues the process of abstraction, and since we classify with words, classification places us on the verbal levels of the abstraction process.

So when people attempt to communicate with one another they automatically leave behind the nonverbal levels of abstraction. And we continue to abstract (select) fewer and fewer features of the individual as we move from one level to another higher level (from *Brandy* to *beagles* to *dog* to *animal* to *living creature*). The process of abstraction, however, works not only in daily conversations but in many daily activities. Above all, this process should not be thought of as some dark mystery. It is something that is going on around us constantly. Journalist Donald M. Schwartz offers an example of the selection done by the news reporter, noting that the process has already begun by the time the newspaperman or newspaperwoman arrives on the scene: "Laymen generally seem to think reporters go out and cover events—events happening and observable. All too often, though, especially for the regular beat reporter, that isn't true; he merely reports words about other words, spoken or written." Schwartz makes his point by following step by step the report of an ordinary automobile accident:

> The policeman goes to the accident after it happens, listens to the stories of the two drivers, who are too scared and involved at best to tell much of what went on, and usually are interested in presenting only the facts that prove 'it was the other guy's fault.' The cop also may talk to witnesses if any are available. He takes notes on what he thinks he hears, returns to the station,

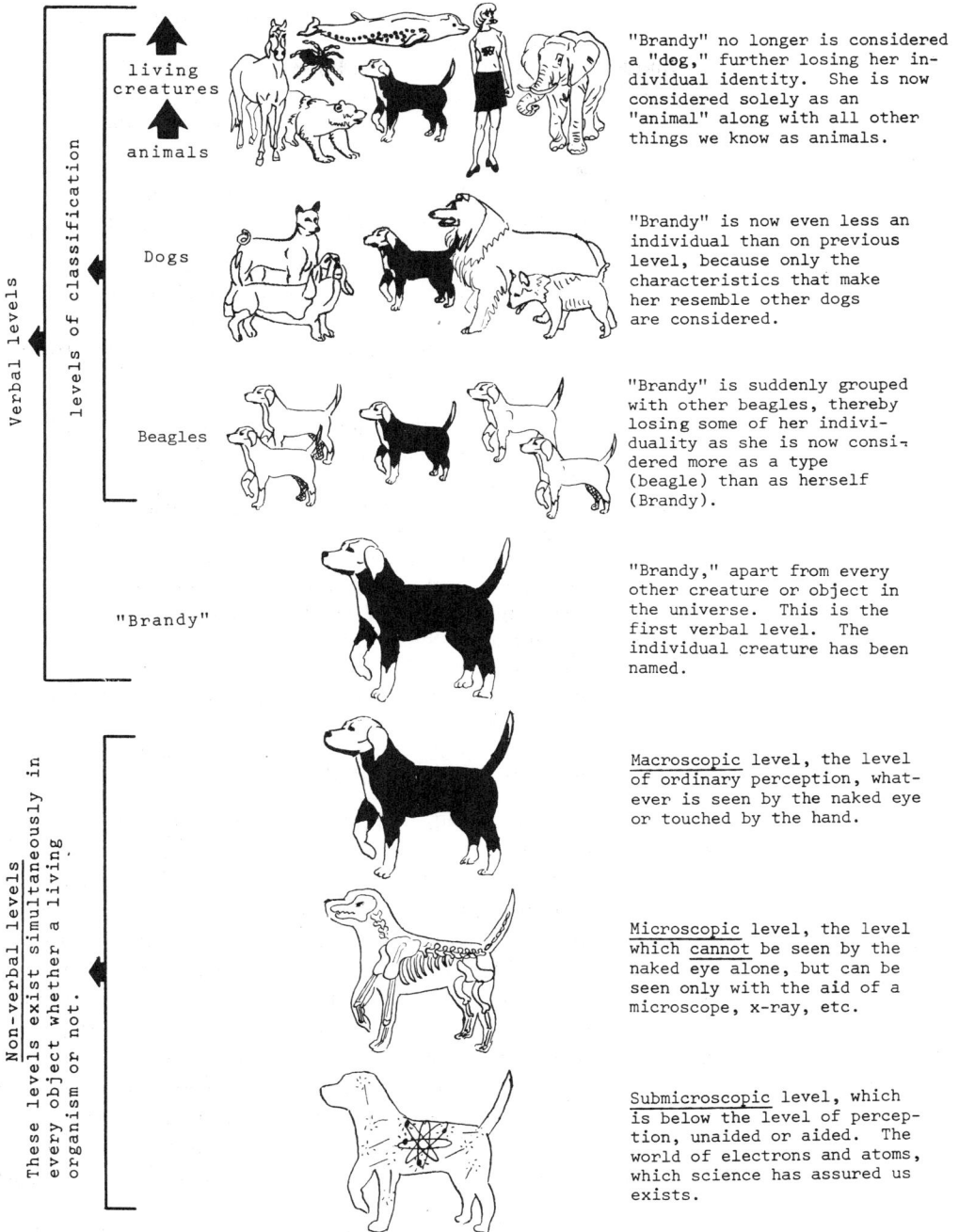

levels of classification

living creatures

animals

"Brandy" no longer is considered a "dog," further losing her individual identity. She is now considered solely as an "animal" along with all other things we know as animals.

Dogs

"Brandy" is now even less an individual than on previous level, because only the characteristics that make her resemble other dogs are considered.

Beagles

"Brandy" is suddenly grouped with other beagles, thereby losing some of her individuality as she is now considered more as a type (beagle) than as herself (Brandy).

"Brandy"

"Brandy," apart from every other creature or object in the universe. This is the first verbal level. The individual creature has been named.

Non-verbal levels

These levels exist simultaneously in every object whether a living organism or not.

<u>Macroscopic</u> level, the level of ordinary perception, whatever is seen by the naked eye or touched by the hand.

<u>Microscopic</u> level, the level which <u>cannot</u> be seen by the naked eye alone, but can be seen only with the aid of a microscope, x-ray, etc.

<u>Submicroscopic</u> level, which is below the level of perception, unaided or aided. The world of electrons and atoms, which science has assured us exists.

Courtesy, Dennis Berner

and turns the material over to a records-writing sergeant, who writes up what he wants of it.

Then our ground-man of the radio station or newspaper, the reporter, arrives on the scene—not the scene of the accident, but the police station. Unless he decides to do some digging, the sergeant's report will be the basis of his story.

And more recently (June 1973) in a PLAYBOY Interview* Walter Cronkite of CBS-NEWS said this:

CRONKITE: In television, we can introduce the public to the people who make the news. We can introduce them to the places where the news is made. And we can give them a bulletin service. In those three particulars, we can beat any other news medium. But for the in-depth reporting that's required for an individual to have a reasonably complete knowledge of his world on any given day—of the city and country and state—we can't touch it.

PLAYBOY: There is a famous story that the CBS news director once pasted up your transcript of the *Evening News* onto a dummy of *The New York Times,* and it covered less than the eight columns of the front page.

CRONKITE: Yes. The number of words spoken in a half-hour evening-news broadcast—words spoken by interviewees, interviewers, me, everybody—came out to be the same number of words as occupy two thirds of the front page of the standard newspaper. We are a front-page service. We don't have time to deal with the back pages at all.

The business of selecting, then, continues on the verbal levels of abstraction, and it is on these levels that our communication really depends. We use the verbal levels (language) to help accomplish meaningful communication, to express what we are capable of expressing, to express what we are capable of getting another person to understand. And one of the most useful methods we have for doing this is that of selecting items in the universe, animate or inanimate, which have similar characteristics, grouping them, and giving general names to these groups: tables, dogs, shirts, boys—your choices are nearly endless. It is with this grouping process, *classification*, that we impose an order on the world around us. Without it we would have to have a separate name for every object in the universe, a situation the human mind would be incapable of dealing with. Without classi-

---

* Excerpt from the "Playboy Interview with Walter Cronkite." Originally appeared in PLAYBOY Magazine; copyright © 1973 by Playboy.

fication, meaningful communication would all but disintegrate. After all, you don't have to know the name of a dog to know that it is a dog; we are able to speak about dogs in general without knowing the name of a single one of these creatures. It is this process of grouping, and then naming those groups, that is the key to meaningful human communication.

Classification, then, continues on the verbal levels the process of abstraction we have seen operating on the nonverbal levels. We dismiss a great many unique characteristics about a particular creature that might be trotting along when we speak about *dogs*, just as we leave out a great many characteristics unique to dogs when we speak about *animals*. Put simply, when you group each member is overshadowed and loses its separateness in the process, because it is now recognized only insofar as it resembles something else. This loss of individuality, while something to consider and beware of, is still a small price to pay for the conveniences that classification affords us. (When the grouping obliterates, instead of merely overshadowing the individual, stereotyping results, a process we will examine shortly.)

> Animals are classified in one way by the meat industry, in another way by the leather industry, in another different way by the fur industry, and in a still different way by the biologist. None of these classifications is any more final than any of the others; each of them is useful for its purpose.
> —S. I. Hayakawa

An essential aspect of the *classification* process is recognizing that the selection of like characteristics depends on the interests and wishes of the person who is doing the grouping. Different people will classify the same item differently depending on their particular focus which is, in turn, determined by the purpose of their classification. This is not unusual. Our interests determine our focus in all things: We notice restaurants when we're hungry and clocks when we're in a hurry. My focus shifts markedly, for instance, when I ride my bicycle instead of driving my car through a nearby park. Topography suddenly becomes paramount: I avoid pedaling up steep hills at all costs.

Also, in classifying an item we are dealing with things we see or have seen or have talked about, things we have had experience with (however limited), things we then arbitrarily decide to group and appropriately name. A thing, an item, is not part of a group until we have so placed it and so named it, according to our purposes.

The name of the group includes everything that comes under it, though what comes under it may appear, and in fact be, quite different until they are grouped. Cats and dogs and birds and snakes are quite different—until we group them as *pets*. Suddenly these otherwise diverse creatures are thrown together (grouped) under the same heading (classification). Every domestic creature owned by anyone anywhere now holds some commonality with every other creature thus owned. The parakeet suddenly has something in common with the boa constrictor. *Pets*, then, encompasses an extremely varied bunch of living creatures. But not *all* "living creatures." The classification *living creatures* encompasses the classification *pets*, since all pets are included under the more general classification. Thus, everything included within a group is embraced by the name given to the group. Only more general classifications can become inclusive of less general, more specific classifications.

Suggestions

◄§ Divide into groups of three or four. Each group should pick out two items—one animate and one inanimate—and with each item the group should create levels of abstraction that move from the nonverbal levels through several verbal levels. Mark the levels that will involve classification.

◄§ In groups of three or four, have each person spend a few minutes talking about himself or herself: name, occupation, interests, a few personal opinions about anything in general. While he or she is talking, the other members of the group should take notes on how much grouping the individual does, that is, note how many words are used that name a group rather than a single, particular item. After each person has finished speaking, the group should discuss how many times the person used the process of classification and specifically what was classified. Working with a few such groupings, discuss what additional groupings would be more inclusive (more general) and which would be more specific.

ABSTRACT AND CONCRETE WORDS

Finally, we need to consider the word *abstract* in the more general sense of describing individual words and the objects or concepts to which those words refer.

First, in the most basic and general sense, all words are abstract. Words, as we have already pointed out, are not the things themselves; they are not the things to which they refer. Dealing for the moment primarily with spoken words, they are merely sounds, puffs of air leaving someone's mouth, which incidentally refer to other things; hence, all words are abstract in the same sense that they are not concrete. That is, despite the fact that speech causes air particles to vibrate, thereby creating sound waves which are measurable, they cannot be seen or touched except as lines on a chart readable only by the trained eye, and though they certainly can be heard, their nature is such that once uttered they cannot be grasped by the hand and given back to persons who have said something they wish they hadn't. So words—even with their physical properties— are considered abstract in the same sense that anything which cannot be seen or touched is considered abstract.

In still another sense, certain individual words are considered abstract. They are considered general, as opposed, for instance, to those that are considered specific and concrete.

The degree of concreteness we ascribe to a word depends on the concreteness of the thing to which the word refers. If the word refers to a tree, then the word "tree" is considered concrete. A tree, that is the physical tree, the tree in reality (as opposed to the word, the sound we make), is something we can see, feel, even kick, or lean against just to make sure it's really there.

Other words, however, refer to things not so easy to kick or lean against. *Honor, courage,* and *love* may manifest themselves in physical activity, but again, they are not things which we can bottle and examine at our leisure, nor can they be touched in the physical sense. Kick them and you kick empty space; lean against them and down you go! One such abstraction, "liberty," is bitterly contemplated

Courtesy, Tibor Nagy

by Joe Bonham, the critically wounded basketcase protagonist of Dalton Trumbo's antiwar novel, *Johnny Got His Gun.* Agonizing over the loss of much of his body, he makes some useful distinctions about certain kinds of words: "What the hell does liberty mean anyhow? It's just a word like house or table or any other word. Only it's a special kind of word. A guy says house and he can point to a house to prove it. But a guy says come on let's fight for liberty and he can't show you liberty. He can't prove the thing he's talking about. . . ."

Perhaps Stuart Chase, in *The Tyranny of Words*, helps make the point clear for us when he says, "Final identification is achieved only by pointing to the apple, touching it with the hand, seeing it with the eyes, tasting it with the mouth. . . .". Chase is speaking about the concrete, something we can literally sink our teeth into. "Failing this," he says, "[words] wander into regions where there are no apples, no objects, no acts, and so [words] become symbols for airy chunks of nothing at all." This defines the abstract.

Suggestions

◄§ Create a dialogue that might occur in an everyday encounter which will reflect various levels of abstraction. For example, two people may be sitting at a bar, one looking rather disgusted because he has to wait while his car is worked on at the corner garage. Or perhaps one disapproves of the young man his daughter has been dating. Once the conversation is written, trade papers with the next person and have him or her pick out the levels of classification, paying particular attention to the way the conversation moves back and forth on the verbal levels of abstraction.

◄§ Which of the following two art works is properly called *abstract*? How do you know? That is, what do you know now about the word *abstract* that would properly label one of the paintings *abstract*? In what way can both the print and the painting be said to be abstractions?

Watercolor. Collection of the artist.
Untitled, Helen "Nicky" Bottker, 1971

Print. Collection of the artist.

Untitled, Peter Marcus, 1973

Looking at each one separately, determine whether there are any elements in each which are more abstract than other elements.

Draw a picture of an animal, or a friend, or an inanimate object such as a car, tree, musical instrument, or the chair you are sitting in. Explain how your drawing is an abstraction.

STEREOTYPING

Dear Ann Landers:

Why is it that when you tell someone you are a barmaid they look at you as if you had said, "I am a prostitute"? I enjoy my job very much, get $3 an hour base pay and work from 40 to 48 hours a week. I average anywhere from $75 to $100 a week in tips.

Of course there are drawbacks. I'm on my feet eight hours at a stretch and I must work every night, including holidays. I get no fringe benefits such as vacation pay and insurance. I have to put up with a lot of drunks, block their passes tactfully (so they don't get mad), listen to their troubles and settle their dumb arguments.

I was educated in Europe, speak three languages fluently, type, take dictation and can use office equipment. But when I held a so-called "respectable" job, I couldn't clear more than $90 a week after deductions. This meant I had to share an apartment, drive an old car and wear tacky clothes.

Now I live in a beautiful duplex—alone—drive a new car, have a good wardrobe, give generously to charity and help support my widowed mother. My only problem, Ann, is this: What do I say to people who give me the fish-eye when I tell them I'm a barmaid?

Unduly Sensitive

. . . the stereotype . . . censors out much that needs to be taken into account . . .
—Walter Lippmann

In 1973 Eric Crone became the only Harvard quarterback ever drafted by a National Football League team. "Here I was," said Crone in an interview, "drafted by the Cardinals, and they really kept it quiet at school. But I didn't expect them to publicize it. Football players at Harvard are looked down on by the main student body. At other schools, football players are put on a pedestal. But at Harvard, an athlete is viewed as just an athlete, someone who doesn't have a mind."

This barmaid and football player are examples of people who have been denied their individuality. Whatever unique qualities they have that affirm them as individuals separate and apart from every other individual, whatever else and everything else that they may be, have all been dismissed. It's simple. Our barmaid is a "prostitute," our football player, a "dumb jock." They are, in fact, victims of *stereotyping*.

Stereotyping is the process of drawing conclusions about something or someone on the basis of too little information. If we look again at the levels of classification, we see the usefulness of grouping for the purposes of meaningful human communication. In *stereotyping*, however, the process of grouping becomes a perversion.

Many people, in judging Mr. Smith, react to the label rather than to Mr. Smith.
—Anatol Rapoport

In *stereotyping*, individual difference is obliterated by group identity. In stereotyping, labels are often based on the most superficial observation, such as skin color, religious beliefs, or clothing. All that a person may actually be is shredded and discarded. In G. B. Trudeau's cartoon creation, *Doonesbury*, one of his collection of college students, Mark Slackmeyer, is eager to bring to "unenlightened construction workers" the good word about the revolution, about a beautiful student-worker alliance. The enlightened Mr. Slackmeyer has assumed a great deal when he approaches the particular hardhat in the comic strip seen here.

Stereotypes ignore the normal differences between people, and they ignore the fact that any one person has a complex set of motives, values and behaviors.
—*Judith M. Bardwick*

EXCUSE ME, BUD. CAN I ASK YOU A QUESTION?

SURE.

WHY IS IT YOU CONSTRUCTION WORKERS ARE SO UNENLIGHTENED? DON'T HARDHATS KNOW ANYTHING ABOUT THE MARXIST DOCTRINES?

OH, YEAH, A LITTLE.

BUT I THINK THEY'RE VERY ANACHRONISTIC. I PREFER ANDRÉ MALRAUX'S CONTENTION THAT MARXISM IS NOT A DOCTRINE, BUT A WILL, A WILL TO FEEL PROLETARIAT.

HAND ME ANOTHER BRICK, WILL YA?

In human interaction, stereotyping is classification carried far beyond the useful purposes that grouping serves. Stereotyping negates individuality. It negates the identity and uniqueness that we recognize when each person is given a name. It is on this first verbal level of identity—naming the individual person or object—that so much rests. Yet it is precisely this level and all that this level implies that is so readily overlooked as our prejudices are learned and allowed to fester and affect our actions. Those guilty of stereotyping leap from the macroscopic level of their perception to draw not useful generalizations, but conclusions which too often have not the slightest foundation in fact. It is a phenomenon that allows one human to see another human as one thing and one thing only, or solely as a member of a group, thereby denying the complexity of the world and the people in it.

This is not to say that some cultural stereotypes don't contain an element of "truth." As John Finley Scott and Lois Heyman Scott, writing in the *New York Times Magazine* in 1968 pointed out, "The tragedy of race in this country (and many others) is that visible genetic differences [that is, skin color], superficial in themselves, have become generally reliable clues to a person's class position—his education, his income, his manners." But we seldom deal with whole groups at once; we deal instead with individuals, and in dealing with individuals, stereotypes are usually more misleading than helpful. They may even deny reality. All items are, after all, unique. Each thing in the universe is different from every other thing. But if we allow the stereotype, whatever it may be, to dominate the way we relate to things around us, we lose touch with that reality. If, for example, our favorite puppy snaps at us, we might consider that she is having a bad day. Or we could conclude that all dogs bite and thereby cut ourselves off from the pleasure of their companionship.

All this may seem harsh—unless you happen to be the barmaid or the football player—but stereotyping can take on even more serious and destructive dimensions. In *Black Rage*, psychiatrists William H. Grier and Price M. Cobbs concentrate on the blanket of racism smothering America and fix on the "development of anti-black feeling and a pervasive climate of prejudice which stimulates and evokes the potential of race prejudice in everyone." They focus too on the "set of attitudes about how blacks are to be treated":

A young white man sought treatment after his wife had left him. He was depressed and obsessively recounted the details of his brief marriage. Finally he telephoned his wife and pleaded

> We do not study a man and judge him to be bad. We see a bad man . . . Neither justice, nor mercy, nor truth enter into such a judgment, for the judgment preceded the evidence.
> —Walter Lippmann

with her to return. She was contemptuous, and he shouted: "Goddammit, treat me like a white man!"

Grouping, classification, must remain our convenience, not become our excuse for thoughtless and cruel behavior. The fact that we are different—not better or worse, but different—must be acknowledged if there is to be human understanding, for without such understanding meaningful human communication is, at best, deferred. In 1929 a young, rising United States Army officer named Stilwell insisted on this concept of difference on a broader, international scale in a lecture to his fellow officers at the Infantry School at Fort Benning in Georgia. His lesson is recounted by historian Barbara Tuchman:

> . . . the reason Westerners apply the cliché "inscrutable" to the Chinese is that they find them "different from us." Why are they different? Because having been "cut off" as Stilwell put it, from our civilization [even Stilwell was not free of arrogance], for so many centuries they have developed under different conditions a civilization of their own. "How then can a Chinese be expected to react like a Westerner? . . . Answer, he can't."

Stilwell—later to become Commander of the entire China-Burma-India theater in World War II—added his most poignant comment: "Dignity, then, is their most prized possession and he who strips them of it makes bitter enemies. . . . In dealing with Chinese don't take their face from them unless you want to humiliate them and unless you do not care if you make enemies."

I would add to this last comment only by substituting the word *humans* for the word *Chinese*. Hopes for reduction of stereotyping in the near future rest first with people like Carmen Mayni, appointed in 1973 as Director of the Women's Bureau of the United States Department of Labor, who said, "A woman's place is where she wants to be"; and second, on the man who when asked by a Harris pollster, "Would you want your daughter to marry a Negro?" replied, "Which Negro did you have in mind?"

COFFEE BREAK

Langston Hughes

> "My boss is white," said Simple.
> "Most bosses are," I said.

"And being white and curious, my boss keeps asking me just what does *the* Negro want. Yesterday he tackled me during the coffee break, talking about *the* Negro. He always says '*the* Negro,' as if there was not 50-11 different kinds of Negroes in the U.S.A.," complained Simple. "My boss says, 'Now that you-all have got the Civil Rights Bill and the Supreme Court, Adam Powell in Congress, Ralph Bunche in the United Nations, and Leontyne Price singing in the Metropolitan Opera, plus Dr. Martin Luther King getting the Nobel Prize, what more do you want? I am asking you, just what does *the* Negro want?'

" 'I am not *the* Negro,' I says. 'I am *me*.'

" 'Well,' says my boss, 'you represent *the* Negro.'

" 'I do not,' I says. 'I represent my own self.'

" 'Ralph Bunche represents you, then,' says my boss, 'and Thurgood Marshall and Martin Luther King. Do they not?'

" 'I am proud to be represented by such men, if you say they represent me,' I said. 'But all them men you name are *way* up there, and they do not drink beer in my bar. I have never seen a single one of them mens on Lenox Avenue in my natural life. So far as I know, they do not even live in Harlem. I cannot find them in the telephone book. They all got private numbers. But since you say they represent *the* Negro, why do you not ask them what *the* Negro wants?'

" 'I cannot get to them,' says my boss.

" 'Neither can I,' I says, 'so we both is in the same boat.'

" 'Well then, to come nearer home,' says my boss, 'Roy Wilkins fights your battles, also James Farmer.'

" 'They do not drink in my bar, neither,' I said.

" 'Don't Wilkins and Farmer live in Harlem?' he asked.

" 'Not to my knowledge,' I said. 'And I bet they have not been to the Apollo since Jackie Mabley cracked the first joke.'

" 'I do not know him,' said my boss, 'but I see Nipsey Russell and Bill Cosby on TV.'

" 'Jackie Mabley is no *him*,' I said. 'She is a *she*—better known as Moms.'

" 'Oh,' said my boss.

" 'And Moms Mabley has a story on one of her records about Little Cindy Ella and the magic slippers going to the Junior Prom at Ole Miss which tells all about what the Negro wants.'

" 'What's its conclusion?' asked my boss.

" 'When the clock strikes midnight, Little Cindy Ella is dancing with the President of the Ku Klux Klan, says Moms, but at the stroke of twelve, Cindy Ella turns back to her natural self, black, and her blonde wig turns to a stocking cap—and her trial comes up next week.'

" 'A symbolic tale,' says my boss, 'meaning, I take it, that *the* Negro is in jail. But you are not in jail.'

" 'That's what you think,' I said.

" 'Anyhow, you claim you are not *the* Negro,' said my boss.

" 'I am not,' I said, 'I am *this* Negro.'

" 'Then what do *you* want?' asked my boss.

" 'To get out of jail,' I said.

" 'What jail?'

" 'The jail you got me in.'

" 'Me?' yells my boss. 'I have not got you in jail. Why, boy, I like you. I am a liberal. I voted for Kennedy. And this time for Johnson. I believe in integration. Now that you got it, though, what more do you want?'

" 'Reintegration,' I said.

" 'Meaning by that, what?'

" 'That you be integrated with *me*, not me with you.'

" 'Do you mean that I come and live in Harlem?' asked my boss. 'Never!'

" 'I live in Harlem,' I said.

" 'You are adjusted to it,' said my boss. 'But there is so much crime in Harlem.'

" 'There are no two-hundred-thousand-dollar bank robberies, though,' I said, 'of which there was three lately *elsewhere*—all done by white folks, and nary one in Harlem. The biggest and best crime is outside of Harlem. We never has no half-million-dollar jewelry robberies, no missing star sapphires. You better come uptown with me and reintegrate.'

" 'Negroes are the ones who want to be integrated,' said my boss.

" 'And white folks are the ones who do *not* want to be,' I said.

" 'Up to a point, we do,' said my boss.

" 'That is what *the* Negro wants,' I said, 'to remove that *point*.'

" 'The coffee break is over,' said my boss."

Suggestions

⌐§   In a single paragraph (100–150 words), explain how the people in your neighborhood, or perhaps your high school classmates, would react to this story by Langston Hughes.

This story was published in 1965. In a paragraph of the same length as the one above, tell how you think the attitudes of whites have changed since then. Or have they? How have the attitudes of blacks changed? Or have they?

◄§ How would you compare Dick Gregory's statement, "I am an individual first, an American second, and a Negro third," with certain
statements in this story, such as "I am not *the* Negro. I am me!" or "I
am *this* Negro"?

◄§ The late language and communication expert Irving J. Lee told the
following true story:

> Pete Hatsucko had been born in this country, though one of his
> parents had been born in Japan. He went to the public schools
> and received a degree from the State University. He had never been
> to Japan. He could not read or write Japanese. He knew only a few
> Japanese phrases used in family small talk. After his induction into the
> Army, he was assigned to the infantry. The orientation program in-
> cluded talks on the nature of the enemy. The captain in charge
> thought Pete should give one of the talks on "The Japanese Men-
> tality." Pete tried in all candor to explain that he knew practically
> nothing about Japanese life and culture, that both his and his father's
> education had been received in this country. "But you're a Japanese,"
> argued the captain, "and you know about the Japanese. You prepare
> the talk." Pete did—from notes after he had read an Army handbook
> and a half-dozen popular magazine articles.

In this and the following statement, comments and incidents, discuss
each as it relates to stereotyping. Determine what the circumstances are,
who is stereotyping and in what ways. Also determine the nature of the
stereotype, that is whether it is ignorant, vicious, harmless, or humorous.
In addition, what degree of "truth" do you find in each case? For example,
in recounting the above story, Professor Lee made clear that there was
nothing "sinister" in the captain's thinking. Do you agree or disagree?
Why or why not?

> The underlying assumption seems to be a woman 'should' belong
> to a man, and if she doesn't for too long a time, something is amiss.
> People disapprove of women without men, not in an overt way, but
> by exhibiting a vague, general cautiousness toward what is not known
> or understood (for example neighbors speculating about friendship
> between two female schoolteachers who buy a home together).

—Patricia O'Brien, *The Woman Alone*

Love is the delusion that one woman differs from another.

—H. L. Mencken, *Mencken*

> Women are reared now as they have always been in this country,
> with the spoken and unspoken assumption from the cradle that they
> will marry. . . . In contrast, a man is raised with a sense of what he
> is to be, not whom he is to marry, and he is therefore identified by
> what he does. He is a plumber, or president of the bank. A woman
> is identified by whom she marries—she is the plumber's wife. A
> woman from Alabama, ill, two divorces behind her, put it to me

starkly: 'From the time I was little girl, I knew I was nothing unless I got myself a man.'

—Patricia O'Brien, *The Woman Alone*

Yellow Bear of the Arapahos also agreed to bring his people to Fort Cobb in 1868. A few days later, Tosawi brought in the first band of Comanches to surrender. When he was presented to Sheridan, Tosawi's eyes brightened. He spoke his own name and added two words of broken English. 'Tosawi, good Indian,' he said.

It was then that General Sheridan uttered the immortal words: 'The only good Indians I ever saw were dead.' Lieutenant Charles Nordstrom, who was present, remembered the words and passed them on, until in time they were honed into an American aphorism: *The only good Indian is a dead Indian.*

—Dee Brown, *Bury My Heart at Wounded Knee*

Everything we admire on this earth—science and art, technology and inventions—is only the creative product of a few people and originally perhaps of *one* race. On them depends the existence of this whole culture. If they perish the beauty of this earth will sink into the grave with them. . . . All the human culture, all the results of art, science, and technology that we see before us today, are almost exclusively the creative product of the Aryan.

—Adolf Hitler, *Mein Kampf*

⊷ Read the paragraphs you wrote in which you tried to determine neighborhood reaction to Langston Hughes' short story "Coffee Break." Read too your paragraphs on changes (or lack of them) in attitudes of blacks and whites. Were you guilty of stereotyping? That is, did you use such phrases as "the people" or "the white man" or "the black man"? Would you avoid using these phrases if you were asked to write the paragraphs again? Explain your answer.

⊷ Describe an instance in which you were or someone you know of was guilty of stereotyping. Describe your own example in the way you have been asked to consider the stereotypes above.

DENOTATION, CONNOTATION AND THE DICTIONARY

"I must be frank with you . . . The fact is that one can't stay a dirty old man forever and you will have to face that fact steadily and unafraid. You can be a dirty old man only as long as you live. Once you die, it's over."

This statement from Isaac Asimov's unscientific study leads to

Mainly, language is an instrument for action. The meaning of a word or phrase is not its dictionary equivalent but the difference its utterance brings about in a situation.
—*Clyde Kluckhohn*

many hints on how to become a successful sensuous dirty old man. He establishes early in his book, *The Sensuous Dirty Old Man,* that the eyes are the "prime tool" of such a gentleman. But they must be used correctly—as in the case of the "leer." He then proceeds to draw the critical distinction between the leer as it is practiced and the leer as it is defined in the dictionary. In addition, he incidentally but explicitly shows his distrust of dictionary definitions—or *denotations* —of words, relying instead on *connotation*—the previous associations and personal experiences that each person brings to different words.

Here is what he says:

> . . . there is nothing on which so much misinformation is prevalent as on the leer.
> . . . there are few people who can actually describe what a leer is.
> The answer may surprise you. The leer is a look out of the corner of the eye . . .
> If you don't believe me, look it up in the dictionary.
> This may puzzle you. If the leer is merely a sidewise glance, which I have stigmatized as not only worthless, but actually harmful, how has it come about that it is so highly regarded?
> The difference, you see, is between the dictionary's opinion of what "leer" means and the actual use of the word. After all, the dictionary, you must understand, is a largely useless volume intended to serve as a monument to the language as used in the previous century.
> So ask not what Webster is saying to the American public, ask rather what the American public is saying to Webster . . .
> The fact is that to the general public a "leer" is defined as a "dirty smile." If this is the definition, then a leer is rightly the strongest weapon in the long-distance armory of the dirty old man. What better activity for a dirty old man than a dirty old smile?
>
> And how does one make a smile dirty? . . . By rolling the eyes, raising the eyebrows, clicking the tongue, uttering a 'Wow' and so on.
> In short, what I have been talking about . . . is the leer as practiced by dirty old men . . . not as defined in the dictionary.

As is the case with Dr. Asimov and the "leer," our concern is with the various connotative meanings that every individual brings to a word, but there are things worth noting first about the set denotative (dictionary) meanings of a word, which have narrow limits and tight boundaries.

With *denotation,* there is always at least one meaning for every word, but most words have several meanings. A person's *back*, for example, is different from the *back* of a book, and both are different still from the verb *back*, meaning "to support, as with authority, influence, help, or money." In each case, the sound and spelling of the word are identical, but they are considered different words because they refer to different things. In fact, some of our most common words have a large number of denotative meanings: *around* has over thirty, *back* and *low*, over fifty, *draw*, over sixty, *pass*, over eighty, *hand*, over ninety, and *run*, over one hundred seventy.

These various denotative meanings will vary from context to context, as well as from person to person. The denotative meaning of the word *blitz* will be different to an American or Englishman who suffered amid the horror and rubble of the Nazi saturation bombing of London during World War II, than for an American today, to whom *blitz* is the charge of a safetyman crashing in on an opposing quarterback. In addition, my cardplaying friends tell me *blitz* has still a different meaning for them. *Checking* someone's figures is not the same as *checking* a center iceman into the boards.

Thus, denotative meanings of words which have the same sound and same spelling do *not* always refer to the same thing. Their denotative meanings make them separate words because each, though spelled the same and pronounced the same, refers to different things in the world around us (as in the case of the word *blitz*). Connotative meanings of words, on the other hand, with their different sounds and different spellings—and their accompanying range of associations—*do* refer to the same thing. So different are the associated meanings of the words *lady* and *woman* that any advocate of the *women's* liberation movement would object to it being described as the *ladies'* liberation movement. These two words, with their different sounds and spellings, do refer to the same living creature. So it's the experience we associate with certain words—even when those words refer to the same person or the same group—that makes the difference.

Connotative meanings are fuzzier and more ambiguous than denotative meanings because connotations result from the experience and associations each person brings to a word. These experiences and associations that each one brings to a particular word can never be exactly alike because no two people can share the same circumstances in the same way; no two people are ever impressed in identical ways, even by identical situations.

With *connotation*, then, ask not what meaning the word brings to us, but rather what meaning we bring to the word, which brings us back to Asimov in the first of the following suggestions.

Suggestions

◄§   What meanings and associations (connotations) do you bring to the words "dirty old man"? What meanings and associations (connotations) do you bring to the word "leer"? Have you ever seen a dirty old man? If so, have you ever seen one leer? If such direct contact is limited, where do you get your information?

Have you made any assumptions about the object of the old man's leer? Where do these assumptions come from? Without rereading the selection, describe the object of the old man's leer. Now reread the selection and point specifically to the words that tell you the object of the leer.

When someone says "the dirty old man leered," what weight of associations overwhelms us and where do these associations come from?

◄§   What associations do you make with the word *lady* as opposed to the word *woman*? How might these associations make a difference in calling the movement *women's* liberation instead of *ladies'* liberation?

◄§   Investigate Asimov's contention about the out-of-date nature of dictionaries. Check some dictionaries for the word "longhair." Do the same for the title "Ms." with reference to women.

Does your investigation support or refute Asimov's assumption that the dictionary is "a largely useless volume"? Explain your answer. Can you think of other words that might support or undercut his position?

For instance, in an attempt to produce cheaper and more tender meat, rancher Bud Basolo—after 15 years of experimentation and a thousand attempts—has a healthy herd of cattle–buffalo hybrids (offspring from different species). Various names have been proposed for this new creature, portions of which may soon be found in the supermarket. Look up the proposed names—"cattalo" and "beefalo"—in a few dictionaries. What do you find? What about the name Basolo? How does the result of your investigation relate to Asimov's statement? What does it tell you about language?

◄§   Make a practice of noting words that have changed (or added) meanings, such as "longhair," or words that have not yet been included in any dictionaries. For example, it may be several years before we see the word "chunnel" in a dictionary. The word refers to the tunnel being constructed to connect England and France beneath the English Channel. The chunnel is to be completed sometime in the 1980s.

◄§   What does Asimov mean when he says, "So ask not what Webster is saying to the American public, ask rather what the American public is saying to Webster"? Do you agree? Explain your answer. Do you know of any instances where the American public is saying anything to Webster? For example, thirty miles north of Boston, Massachusetts, is one of this country's oldest harbor towns, Gloucester. Not far from Gloucester Harbor there is a restaurant which has recently changed its name from "Lobster Land" to "Lobsta Land." The change in spelling from "lobster" to "lobsta" is an effort, one would assume, to conform to the way in which the word is actually pronounced by the local citizenry. The word "lobsta," however, does not appear in any dictionary. Do you suppose it ever will? What do you suppose will have to happen before it does?

◄§   Discuss the denotations and connotations of the words in each list below.

body	discuss	body
figure	kibitz	torso
build	converse	carcass
physique	chat	cadaver
anatomy	gossip	remains

◄§   Add words to each list and discuss them.

◄§   In groups of four or five, create a list of words which refer to the same thing but have different connotative meanings. Each group should discuss its list with the rest of the class.

◄§   Choose a single word, and by changing the context in which the word is used, change the meaning of that word. For example, is a blitzing linebacker's attempt to *sack* the opposing quarterback the same *sack* used to carry home groceries? Or how about the suggestion to someone to "*Park* in the *park*"?

◄§   Page 68 is a reproduction of a letter I received urging me to support the "Mustard Seed Festival" to be held in my neighborhood. The "enclosed brochure" spoken of in the letter's opening paragraph explains in depth the various programs operated by the Joint Community Board: the Summer Program of arts, crafts, music, and dance, among other things; the Teenage Program at the recreational center, which is also the base for a food delivery program; the Tutoring Program in reading, language, art, theater, mathematics, and science; the Neighborhood School, which runs from preschool through the eighth grade; the Senior Citizens Program; the Redevelopment Program, and so on.

Read the letter, paying particular attention initially to the "categories of support" open to contributors. Would you rather be referred to as a *Friend, Sponsor, Patron,* or *Benefactor*? In what particular situation? Can you explain why? What seems to give one increased value over the other or others? Though the words *help* and *donors* are used, *Helper* and *Donor* are not categories. Could they have been? Why or why not?

Write a similar letter urging people to contribute to a similar community project, naming the festival, the community board, and the associations involved. Try to include what would be in an accompanying brochure and assume you have the agreements and resources that the "Mustard Seed Festival Committee" has. Most important, make up your own four categories of support and be able to explain to the class why you have so named each one.

◄§   Create a short dialogue or recreate an actual situation that you

MUSTARD SEED FESTIVAL

Joint Community Board   Trinity Episcopal Church
600 N. Euclid, St. Louis 63108   Second Presbyterian Church
                                         First Unitarian Church

Dear Friend,

The enclosed brochure tells of the pressing needs of the youth programs which have been operated for years by the Joint Community
Board. The fate of summer programs is uncertain due to drastic cuts
in available federal funds.

The Joint Board welcomed the opportunity to join with the Maryland
Plaza Association, the Central West End Association and the Chase
to sponsor the Mustard Seed Festival, a street festival on Maryland
Plaza, Wednesday July 11th.

The day begins with the opening of the shops along Maryland and
Euclid; the Maryland Plaza Association has pledged 10% of the day's
receipts to our neighborhood youth programs.

At 2 p.m. the streets will be closed; offerings will include food
and beverages, art and crafts shows, children's games and crafts,
drama, jazz, bake sales, and movies. Proceeds from these activities go to the Joint Community Board youth programs.

At 8 p.m. the St. Louis Symphony will provide a suitable finale to
an exciting day with Walter Susskind conducting the last of a series
of free community concerts.

The activites of the Festival will serve many purposes in addition
to raising vitally needed money--involvement of all segments of the
community, fun for our neighbors and friends, and publicity for the
activities and needs of the Joint Board. But the Mustard Seed Festival will not of itself raise the $52,000 we seek. We need con-
cerned, caring citizens of our community and city who are willing to
give as much as they can to assist our young people.

What better investment can anyone make? Please help, and join us
for the Festival and the Symphony performance. A special seating
section will be reserved for donors. There are four categories of
support open to you:

                    Friend $ 5-49
                    Sponsor   50-99
                    Patron   100-499
                    Benefactor   500 and above
Checks should be made to the "Joint Community Board." All contributions are tax-deductible.

remember in which the two people misunderstood each other because they attached different meanings to the same word. Was the misunderstanding over denotative or connotative meanings? Explain.

◄§ It is interesting to recall that when the "Founding Fathers" gathered in Philadelphia in 1787 to abolish the Articles of Confederation and write a Constitution, one of the first problems they faced was what to call George Washington, who had been chosen to lead the country. Before finally deciding on *Mr. President*, they kicked around the following titles: the Protector; His Excellency; His Mightiness; the President of the United States. Discuss the connotation of each of these titles and why you think the terms other than *President* were rejected.

EUPHEMISM

> Euphemisms are to the tongue what novocain is to the gums.
> —*Stefan Kanfer*

Closely related to connotation is *euphemism*. As we have previously suggested, our experiences and associations with words dictate what our emotional response to them will be. Particular words will stimulate pleasant or uncomfortable reactions. If our experience is favorable, the word is favorable. A policeman's emotional response to being called *officer* will hardly be the same as his or her response to being called *pig*.

Euphemism is an attempt to manipulate the individual's emotional response. Euphemisms abound and carry with them an inherent danger: whatever sounds okay seems okay—or at least is passively accepted. For example, a club of *limited membership* would not admit that it is *restricted*. And those who *entered* the Watergate complex prior to the 1972 presidential election did not *break in* or *burglarize*; they *penetrated* the building with *human resources*. Others did not *spy* but engaged in *negative campaigning* by becoming *sources of information*.

Writing in *Time* magazine in August 1973, Stefan Kanfer said, "In the [Senate Watergate] hearings, criminality is given scores of numbing disguises. For 'intelligence-gathering operations' read 'breaking and entering,' for 'plumbers' read 'burglars,' for 'stroking' read 'cheap flattery,' for 'puffing' read 'expensive flattery,' for 'White House horrors' read 'Government-sponsored crimes!' . . . All perform the same function: the separation of words from truth."

Journalist Harold K. Mintz has taken a close look at the euphemism boom that has occurred since the early 1960s and its impact on our society.

PLAYING WITH WORDS

Harold K. Mintz
in *Quill*, a Magazine for Journalists

Euphemisms dehumanize people, fog up communications, and sugar-coat the harsh facts of life. They make a simple idea sound much more complicated and important than it really is. Also, they show up in the press all the time.

Since the early 1960s, the use of euphemisms has mushroomed, perhaps to reflect the problems torturing this country. Where there used to be only a handful of euphemisms—pass away for die, social disease for syphilis, plant food for manure, building superintendent for janitor—there are now dozens impinging on many spheres of life. This prevalence of euphemisms applies equally to the armed forces, government and politics, business and labor. Countless generals, bureaucrats, politicians, sociologists, business executives and labor leaders prefer words of Latin origin to Anglo-Saxon words, polysyllabic tongue twisters to one-syllable words. They would rather impress you than inform you.

The Vietnam war has given the military an opportunity to spawn several vague, abstract euphemisms that camouflage the human suffering underneath. When our armed forces destroy forests and farm crops, this action is dignified by either of two euphemisms: "defoliation" or "resource denial program."

Here are other examples, all related to the Vietnam war:

Free fire zone—shoot anything that moves, man, woman, or child.

Protective reaction strike—a bomb raid.

Pacification—bombardment of defenseless villages.

Armed reconnaissance—operations in which pilots are allowed to attack any targets.

Incursion—invasion.

Two other military euphemisms, not linked to Vietnam, deserve mention. Biological weapons, now outlawed, were always referred to as *biological agents*, an almost beneficent-sounding expression. The second euphemism concerns the word *retreat*. Our armed forces have never acknowledged the existence of that word. Consequently, when our Army or Navy backs up in battle, we do not retreat, we engage in a *strategic withdrawal* or a *retrograde action*.

These euphemisms do not prevent the GIs in retreat from being *eliminated with extreme prejudice*, but they do assuage the fears of the folks back home. And it is, after all, these folks whose taxes finance the flexing of military muscle.

Depending on your view of the Vietnam war, young men who avoided induction were either *draft dodgers* or *war resisters,* a much more complimentary term.

When a government behind the Iron Curtain kills or executes a dissident citizen, he is *purged* or *liquidated.* When a government murders tens of thousands of people, that is genocide, a cold, impersonal, bureaucratic type of word. President William McKinley described our brutal subjugation of the Filipinos as *benign assimilation.*

A highly successful lobbyist in the Massachusetts statehouse refers to his endeavors as *social engineering.* How did the highway lobby and the National Rifle Association lobby ever miss out on that winner?

Getting laid off is sometimes a *dehiring* process that involves getting *surplussed* or *temporarily furloughed pending recall.* Carpenters, plumbers, welders, sheet metal workers, etc., no longer wear overalls or work uniforms; they wear career apparel.

At executive conferences scheduled this year by the National Management Association, cocktail hours are passé; they are now *attitude adjustment* periods. Mercury in tuna is a contaminant that the tuna industry plays down as a *microconstituent.*

The annual slaughter of baby seals in Alaska was sweetened up as the *seal harvest* by Maurice Stans, the Secretary of Commerce, in 1971.

Door-to-door selling is humdrum work for clods, but *multilevel merchandising* is for executive trainees about to scale the business ladder. Industrial espionage is dirty pool, but *competitive intelligence* is a challenging and character-building activity.

The current language of sociology abounds with "in" words that are mostly euphemisms. Urban planners and sociologists refer to slum dwellers, for example, as *culturally deprived* (uneducated) and *financially disadvantaged* (poverty-stricken), and the slums as *depressed areas* or *inner cities.* A large number of slum dwellers are *senior citizens* (aged people) enjoying themselves in the *sunset of life,* their *golden years* (very often sick and lonely, at the end of the line).

And clinging to most inner cities are generous layers of dirt, smoke and soot—*particulate pollution.* From these inner cities comes the lion's share of the population of our *correctional institutions* (prisons).

How invigorating it would be to return to the salty, no-nonsense language of Harry Truman. There was no double-talk or forked tongue when he said, "If you can't stand the heat, get out of the kitchen."

Suggestions

❧   Can you think of a situation where you have been involved in "sugar-coating" the facts? Recreate the situation.

❧   What does Mintz mean when he says that "they would rather impress you than inform"? Gather some instances from the media where an individual's or group's idea was to impress rather than inform. Discuss them with the class. Are there any personal instances from your daily contact with others where the idea was to impress rather than inform? Write about them *in your journal* and discuss them with the class. Create a situation where you are the individual who feels forced to impress rather than inform.

❧   Mintz says that depending on a person's point of view those who avoided induction were either draft dodgers or war resisters. It seems then, that one person's euphemism is another person's hard fact. The war fought in this country from 1861 to 1865 is variously known as the Civil War, War of Rebellion, War Between the States, or War of Secession. How do these various names reflect personal points of view? What differences in viewpoint are expressed by the terms applied to the "disturbances" that occurred in certain areas (such as Watts) of various American cities during the 1960s? Were they riots or rebellions?

Can you think of any circumstance where what is a euphemism to one person might be fact to another? For example, what prison inmates call *the hole*, prison officials call *disciplinary segregation*.

Mintz makes the point that euphemisms have "mushroomed, perhaps to reflect the problems torturing this country." Do you think this applies to all euphemisms? Are there any that serve a useful purpose? Can you give some examples?

Lancet, a British medical journal, reported that a British scientist recently conducted an experiment dealing with the "long-term negative health consequences" that nonsmokers suffer from their proximity to smokers. The scientist placed a dozen nonsmokers in a small room filled with smoke from cigars and cigarettes. After an hour, there was an increase in the amount of carbon monoxide in the blood of these nonsmokers. Though the increase was admittedly small, the team of scientists felt it was indicative of damage that can occur in the nonsmoker.

The scientists conceded that the small room contained more smoke than one would likely encounter, but added that "even with slightly better ventilation three or four hours in a smoky car or pub would almost certainly involve a nonsmoker in significant passive smoking."

A Tennessee newspaper took exception (should I say attacked?) the use of the words "passive smoking," calling them a couple of "weasel words," saying that to describe forced inhaling of another person's cigarette or cigar smoke deserved a more direct term, "enforced smoking" or at least "involuntary smoking."

And in what were apparently similar tests in the United States, smoking was marked as the most dangerous way of polluting the air. In buses, autos, planes, and elevators, these tests concluded, non-smokers inhaled as much smoke as the puffers themselves. The result in some cases was serious damage to the heart and lungs. The United States Surgeon General, Jesse L. Steinfeld, insisted that "smoking in the presence of nonsmokers may be considered an act of aggression."

Suggestions

◄§ Do you agree with the newspaper that "passive smoking" is a phrase made up of "weasel words"? What about the phrases suggested by the newspaper? Are they direct enough? Why or why not? How would this newspaper be likely to react to the United States Surgeon General's remark? Is the newspaper's term "weasel words" direct enough? Explain your answer. Give the denotative and connotative meanings of *weasel*. Is the term *passive*, as it is used by the British scientist, related to *pacification* as it was used by the military in the article by Harold Mintz? If so, how? If not, why not?

◄§ Write a short paragraph in which you attack or defend the use of the phrase "passive smoking," making a suggestion or two about comparable phrases (if you are defending) or different phrases (if you are attacking).

Do the same, this time commenting on the United States Surgeon General's phrase "an act of aggression."

◄§ Make a practice of jotting down euphemisms as you hear others use them or as you use them yourself. Describe *in your journal* the circumstances surrounding their use and the effect each had on the particular situation. For example, *Time* Magazine noted that in the six months preceding the signing of the peace agreement in Paris during January 1973, casualties in Vietnam totaled 80,000. In the six months following the signing, reported *Time*, casualties totaled 72,000. When Canada, part of the International Commission of Control and Supervision, finally decided that their task was hopeless and decided to leave, Major General Duncan McAlpine, the Canadian Commander said, "There is no cease-fire. It is an illusion." By contrast, a perpetually optimistic official reportedly claimed, "It's not a cease-fire, it's a less-fire." The only thing left to ask is whether or not the term *less-fire* can accurately describe 72,000 casualties or whether it is "novocain to the mind."

There are other examples, less depressing: Houston's Mission Control tried to convince the Skylab Two astronauts that their motion sickness was really only a little "stomach awareness." Compile your own as you come across them.

DIALECTS

A word needs to be said about dialects and this is it: there are *differences* in the ways people speak.

Not better ways. Not worse ways. Just different ways.

And since we are not likely to ever eliminate those differences, it makes sense to eliminate the value judgments that accompany variations we hear in pronunciation, grammar, and vocabulary, variations which occur not only from dialect to dialect but from person to person. In fact, they differ to the extent that it can be said that each speaker has a separate dialect. A person's speech is considered even more individual and more complex than a set of fingerprints. It is even true that no person ever pronounces the same word in precisely the same way. Though the human ear is not capable of making such fine distinctions, instruments which give a visible picture of a person's speech, sound spectrographs, show us the difference.

Professor James Funkhouser has defined dialect as:

> a variety of a language, set off from other varieties by differences in pronunciation, grammar and vocabulary. Different dialects of a language are, for the most part, mutually understandable. When the variation is so pronounced between the systems that understanding is not possible, then different languages occur.

The negative connotations associated with dialect are decidedly undeserved, but certainly not new. Even the Greeks of the classical period, while not necessarily holding "barbarians" in contempt, did divide the human community between those who spoke Greek (the Hellenes) and those who didn't (the barbarians).

But despite the fact that a particular dialect is *not* a corruption of the language of which it is a part, it is often treated as such. As it happens, as it has happened historically, there develops a "prestige" dialect, a particular variety of the language which comes to be spoken around a center of economic, political, cultural, and social power. In England, London would be such an area; in France, Paris. In America in the last century the Boston and Cambridge area of Massachusetts was one such center; Charleston and Philadelphia were others. The urbanization produced by the Industrial Revolution created new centers of influence along the routes of the westward movement.

Then as now, no single area could claim dominance as *the* center of economic and political power, and of cultural and social prestige. Nevertheless, dialects spoken outside these centers are sneered at and frowned upon, despite the fact that

> [w]hat is true of different races and countries is true also, though in a milder way, of different sections of the same country. There is no nation, so far as I am aware, in which all the citizens or even all the educated citizens use precisely the same speech. Compare the German of Berlin with the German of Munich, the Italian of Naples with the Italian of Florence, the Russian of Odessa with the Russian of Petrograd. And just as the world is more interesting and more intellectually alluring because of the existence of foreign languages, *so our national life is more interesting, more amusing because of the sectional differences of American speech.* [Italics mine]

. . . we shudder over missing *s*'s; missing *ed*'s turn us pale. Why? Are we really incapable of understanding "two boy"? Do we think it's only one? If someone tells us that last night the house "burn" down, do we really not know when it happened?
—*Elisabeth McPherson*

Warnings against emphasizing a presumed superiority of one dialect over any other are not new. This one, as a matter of fact, was sounded in 1917 by Fred Newton Scott, president of the Modern Language Association from 1907 to 1908, and first president of the National Council of Teachers of English from 1911 to 1913.

The extent, however, to which Scott's warning has been ignored is evidenced by the fact that the Convention on College Composition and Communication felt compelled to adopt the following statement in 1974 at its annual gathering:

> We affirm the students' right to their own patterns and varieties of language—the dialects of their nurture or whatever dialects in which they find their own identity and style. Language scholars long ago denied that the myth of a standard American dialect has any validity. The claim that any one dialect is unacceptable amounts to an attempt of one social group to exert its dominance over another. Such a claim leads to false advice for speakers and writers, and immoral advice for humans. A nation proud of its diverse heritage and its cultural and racial variety will preserve its heritage of dialects. We affirm strongly that teachers must have the experience and training that will enable them to respect diversity and uphold the right of students to their own language.

Here we have it, professionals speaking to their colleagues, urging again what Scott had pleaded for a half century before: "When we deal with American speech [Scott said] we shall do well to cultivate the virtue of tolerance."

Suggestions

~§   Members of the class who wish to should point out peculiarities of their own speech. I, for instance, pronounce *wash* in such a way that it sounds as if I pronounce it with an *r*. I *warsh* the dishes after a meal; the capital of the United States is *Warshington*, D.C. Consider the harm done by having people pronounce *wash* as if it were *warsh*. Discuss variations within the class of pronunciation, grammar, and vocabulary.

~§   Teacher Barbara Dodds Stanford has made this statement on dialect:

> Some people argue that the best method of ending linguistic discrimination would be to teach everyone the same dialect. In that case, wouldn't the most effective method of ending racial discrimination be to dye everyone's hair black and skin brown? And religious discrimination could be ended by having everyone adopt a combination of Catholicism, Methodism, Pentecostalism, with perhaps a sprinkling of Buddhism and Voodoo. And as for proposals to eliminate discrimination by sex, I hate to imagine!
>
> Conformity is not admired in other areas of life, so why should we deprive ourselves of the richness and variety of language that dialects provide us? Equality does not come by eliminating those that are different or even just the differences. Black people are only asking for the basic human right to respect themselves when they reject hair straighteners and bleaching creams. And I am convinced that the inability of children to learn a simple verb conjugation in 12 years is not the result of stupidity, but a healthy subconscious refusal to deny a part of themselves. Freedom is not real if it is simply the freedom to conform to everyone else. Freedom is only real if it guarantees to everyone the right to be himself, to look like himself, and to speak like himself.

In your journal and then with the class, compare the freedom spoken of in this statement with the kind of freedom implied in the song "Imagine," by John Lennon. What kind is each talking about? Would their definitions be different or similar? Explain. Do you agree or disagree with one or both about what constitutes freedom? Explain your answer.

4 Language and Thought: The Limits of Language

Language has limits. These limits are evident not only between people of different cultures but between people of the same culture.

Even within one culture, for example, a person's feelings, thoughts, and dreams cannot be fully transferred to another person. Neither can love or pain be appreciated in precisely the same way by two different human nervous systems. One person cannot feel another person's toothache no matter how sympathetic the person with the healthy teeth may be. The best that that healthy friend can do is remember what it was like when he or she suffered in a similar situation.

These limits occur, then, even between people who speak the same language. The problems are compounded, of course, when two people speak different languages and are from significantly different cultures. In an extensive study of the Navaho Indian culture, anthropologist Clyde Kluckhohn and physician Dorothea Leighton concluded that each language "is a different system of categorizing and interpreting experience." In their book, *Navaho*, in a chapter entitled "The Tongue of People," they describe how different the Navaho view is from our own on something as basic as hunger. To the Navaho hunger is something to which the individual is subjected by an outside force; it is not something within the individual. Indeed if a Navaho-speaking American is pressed for an explanation of this linguistic idiom, he is likely to say, "The spirit of hunger sits here beside me." An English-speaking American, however, sees hunger as an internal physical condition and is likely to say, "I *am* hungry. I haven't eaten since breakfast."

In the 1930s and 1940s, an insurance businessman with an interest in language, Benjamin Lee Whorf, developed the theory that language is neither the tool nor the mere reflection of thinking, but

77

instead channels the thought processes and determines how we look at the universe around us. Whorf did not see language as something distinct from thinking. In his view, language is not simply the tool we use to impart information to someone else. He believed instead that language precedes and directs a person's thinking.

Whorf came to these conclusions not by studying French, German, Greek, Russian, or Iranian or Hindustani—all of which are related to English and to each other as members of the Indo-European family of languages—but by studying the American Hopi language and the Aztec language, both as unrelated to English as is Chinese.

The question Whorf raised is how do different languages treat nature, which, he insisted, is only "artificially isolated" into parts. Whorf would have us remember that nature is *not* divided into neat parts; we break it into parts by the words and the structure of our language. Our language leads us to classify what we see according to our own system. For instance, we include creatures as different as sparrows and ostriches as members of the same group (birds) and forget that we might classify by other methods, by size, perhaps, instead of by their ability to lay eggs. If size were our way of grouping, then butterflies and sparrows—two little creatures that fly—would belong together in one group; ostriches would fit with some other group, larger animals that don't fly. If we grouped living creatures according to the number of bones in the neck, whales, giraffes, humans, and mice would be lumped together since each has seven. And our notion of "life," and thus feeling or "spirit," applies only to things with breath and conscious movement, not—as in some languages—to rocks and rivers and clouds.

Even more important than our use of words to classify, however, is the structure of the language, the pattern into which we fit the words. English, for instance, operates on a subject-verb system. The *doer* (subject) *does* something (the verb). It seems as if there must be a "doer" making things happen, whether the doer is a person or a natural phenomenon. Stuart Chase, in his "How Language Shapes Our Thoughts," describes the distinctions made by Whorf: "In English we say, 'The light flashed,'" explains Chase. "Something has to be there to make the flash; 'light' is the subject, 'flash' the predicate." In other words, the light *made* the flash. Modern physics, however, tends to emphasize the idea of *field* and is moving away from seeing the universe in terms of subject (doer) and predicate (the thing done). As Chase says, Hopi speakers are better physicists when they say *Reh-pi—flash*—in a single word, than we are when we insist on saying *something flashes*, and then add the time element our language won't let us avoid: *flashes* right now, or *flashed* at some earlier time. As Whorf himself said, "English and similar tongues lead us to think of the universe as a collection of rather distinct objects and events corresponding to words." He believes that people whose languages are as diverse as English, Hopi, and Chinese, will see the world from different viewpoints, that their thought patterns will vary according to their language. Other languages, Whorf said, "which do not paint the separate-object picture of the universe to the same degree as English and its sister tongues, point toward possible new types of logic and possible new cosmical pictures."

> Thinking is a matter of different tongues.
> —B. L. Whorf

Suggestions

◄§   *Light, chair, sky, horse, self, rain, group*—these words are names of things. They all seem to name parts of our world. But try the following: turn the light switch off (or if it is already off, turn it on). Repeat this a few times. Now stop and think a while. Where does the light go when you turn it off? Where is it (besides in the bulb) when you have it on? Now return to the list of words. Do they name parts of your world in the same way they did before? Do they, in fact, name parts of your world at all, or do they just name aspects of your perception?

◄§   In a recent book of essays, *The Lives of a Cell, Notes of a Biology Watcher*, scientist Lewis Thomas contemplates his own idea of a possible new cosmical picture. He talks of how humans must cope with

> . . . the dawning, intensifying realization of just how interlocked [with nature] we are.
> A good case can be made for our nonexistence as entities. We are not made up, as we had always supposed, of successively enriched packets of our own parts. We are shared, rented, occupied. At the interior of our cells, driving them, providing the oxidative energy that sends us out for the improvement of each shining day, are the mitochondria [a minute body occurring in the cytoplasm of cells], and in a strict sense they are not ours. They turn out to be little separate creatures [without whom] we would not move a muscle, drum a finger, think a thought.

Dr. Thomas draws some conclusions from this:

> The uniformity of the earth's life, more astonishing than its diversity, is accountable by the high probability that we derived, originally, from some single cell, fertilized in a bolt of lightning as the earth cooled. It is from the progeny of this parent cell that we take our looks; we still share genes around, and the resemblance of the enzymes of grasses to those of whales is a family resemblance.

I have been trying to think of the earth as a kind of organism, but it is no go. I cannot think of it this way. It is too big, too complex, with too many working parts lacking visible connections. The other night, driving through a hilly, wooded part of southern New England, I wondered about this. If not like an organism, what is it like, what is it *most* like? Then, satisfactorily for that moment, it came to me: it is *most* like a single cell.

Take some time to think about Thomas's cosmic picture; it differs markedly from the one most of us share. How would this cosmic viewpoint affect the language you use? Would it change the structure? Would it change the words in use?

Now take some time to think out your own new cosmic picture. Describe it *in your journal* and discuss it with the class. How would your picture affect the structure and words of the language you use? Suppose, for instance, that my view of the cosmos saw what we call the ground and everything that emanated *naturally* from it as one huge, variously shaped, connected mass. Would I then have a word for what we call a *tree?* or *mountain?* or *hill?* or *grass?* Explain your answer.

Not everyone, however, agrees with Whorf that the language we grow up speaking controls the way we think. Other language experts say Whorf's theories are plausible but not proven. Culture and the surrounding reality (the environment), they say, influence a person's language. They account for the differences in languages by pointing to the differences in environment and cultures.

The Hopi, Whorf told us, use the same word to name everything that flies—except birds—whether a pilot, an airplane, or an insect. To divide things in any other way would be "unthinkable," in the same way that it would be unthinkable for an Eskimo to describe snow as we do in a single word. We don't ordinarily distinguish between falling snow, slushy snow, wind-driven snow, and so on. To the Eskimo, however, these different kinds of snow would be "sensuously and operationally different, different things to contend with; [the Eskimo] uses different words for them and for other kinds of snow." On the other hand, the Eskimos are likely to use a single word—machines—for the many complicated devices we have for doing our work for us: lathes, for instance, and drill presses and assembly lines and computers. We have one main word, *snow*, and sometimes a second—*blizzard*—but other languages, Aztec, for instance, tend to lump together snow and ice and cold as a single thing, a thing not very important to them. In an environment where snow fell very seldom, if at all, the Aztecs didn't care much about the way it differed from ice. But in an environment where recognizing subtle qualities of snow can affect daily survival, the language acknowledges that importance with an array of terms.

To Whorf, these distinctions are the dictates of language; to those less convinced by the Whorfian theory, such distinctions—or lack of them (as with the Hopi Indians and flying objects or the Aztecs and ice or snow)—are the dictates imposed by the reality of the environment.

In Arabic, there are more than six thousand words for a camel and its parts and equipment. How many could the average American name? And why would we care? Are these differences the influence of language or the necessity of environment?

It's fairly easy to see how the *words* in a language are affected by where we live and what is important to us; it's more complicated to understand how the structure of the language—the way the words are strung together—can, as Clyde Kluckhohn and Dorothea Leighton say, have "an effect upon what the people who use it see, what they feel, how they think, what they can talk about."

Linguistics Professor Ronald Langacker disagrees with Whorf, Kluckhohn, and Leighton, saying that "[t]here is absolutely no reason to believe that the grammatical structure of our language holds our thoughts in a tyrannical vice-like grip." These two statements are not as nearly mutually exclusive as they may at first appear. Both are valid to some extent. Kluckhohn and Leighton admit that "[a]lmost anything which can be said in Navaho can be said in English and vice versa, though [he is quick to point out] a translation which gets everything in may take the form of a long paraphrase which sounds strained and artificial in the second language." They note that certain distinctions made in one language are not consistently made in another. English speaking people report rain in a number of ways: "It has started to rain," or "It has stopped raining," or "It is raining." The Navaho, say Leighton and Kluckhohn, convey the same ideas, but with finer variations. The Navaho

uses one verb form if he himself is aware of the actual inception of the rain storm, another if he has reason to believe that rain has been falling for some time in his locality before the occurrence struck his attention. One form must be employed if rain is generally round about within the range of vision; another if, though it is raining round about, the storm is plainly on the move. Similarly, the Navaho must invariably distinguish between the ceasing of rainfall (generally) and the stopping of rain in a particular vicinity because the rain clouds have been driven off by wind.

Suggestions

◄§   Look carefully at a color spectrum. Where does "blue" end and "purple" begin? Where does "purple" end and "red" begin?

Make up a name for that color we call yellow-green. We call it yellow-green because, of course, it looks like a combination of those two colors, but we need a new word in order to give it its own integrity and its own identity. Now you have a new color—not a mere combination of two colors. Thus, you have yellow as a lighter shade and green as a darker shade of the new color. Yellow, then, is light _____; green is a dark _____. What does this do to the status of yellow and green as distinct colors?

Could the color divisions be drawn in different places than our language tells us to draw them?

◄§   Years ago *harness* and *livery stable* were common words. So were *scrubboard, ashpit,* and *bustle.* Why have they almost disappeared from the language? What other words are no longer in common use?

◄§   What words or groups of words are familiar to most Americans that probably do not exist in Cherokee? in Polynesian? in Chinese? Do you happen to know any words from these cultures that would be unfamiliar to most Americans?

For our purposes, however, we need not argue the validity of Whorf's theory. Whether differences exist because language influences how people of distinctly different cultures see the world around them is less important to us than recognizing *that differences in language do indeed exist, and that people of different cultures do view the world in different ways.*

We get a better look at some of these interesting differences by comparing our own language to others. Chinese, for instance, is a more *relative* language than ours. That is, the Chinese do not usually deal in absolutes, as English speakers do. In English, we say that *something is something,* as in "The car is long." English, generally, allows us to make two kinds of statements: the subject and verb structure we've already talked about (doer + something done); or an "equals" statement, something *is* (equals) something. To the Chinese, however, saying that the car *is* long makes no sense; it is unacceptable. "Long" does not exist as something so utterly independent; it is not a quality all its own. In Chinese, Stuart Chase points out, "the long and the short are mutually related; the difficult and easy are mutually complementary; the front and the rear mutually accompanying." These qualities—front/rear, long/short, difficult/easy— are relative, not absolutes in themselves. One can always ask, "where does the *rear* stop and the *front* begin," or "*long* in comparison to what?" or, "*difficult* compared to what?" and so on. As Chase puts it: "In the West we say, 'This is the front of the car, and that is the rear, and let's have no more nonsense about it!' But in the Chinese view, Westerners are guilty of considerable nonsense in creating 'frontness' and 'rearness' as entities. Even a Westerner can see that if a car is torn in two in a crash, the part with the radiator grille becomes the 'front,' and the part toward the now severed windshield becomes the 'rear'—*of that segment.*"

The culprit is *is*. Our use of *is* has a lot to do with our giving qualities such as *front* and *back*, *blue* and *red*, and *large* and *small* such definite and absolute equality by themselves, somewhere out there.

When we say that something *is* something—"The curtain is blue," or "The Mayor is honest"—we ignore the relative nature of *blueness* and of *honesty* and talk as though there existed somewhere an absolute blue, and a universal and permanent set of behavior that everybody would agree constituted honesty. In denying the relative nature of things—something the Chinese mind would not do—we deny the part that our own nervous system, our own senses, or our own experiences, play in perceiving objects or behavior. As artist Josef Albers has pointed out, "If one says 'red' and there are fifty people listening, it can be expected that there will be fifty reds in their minds. And one can be sure that these reds will all be very different." Thus, to say that "The curtain is blue" establishes the color *blue* as something that exists entirely independent of our perception of it. To say that "The Mayor is honest" assumes a general agreement that taking a stamp from the city to mail a personal letter is honest, accepting a bribe from the phone company is not.

What we need to do is to recognize that these "qualities" (even labelling them as "qualities" gives them an independence they should not have), like *blue* for example, are valid only insofar as we recognize that they are what Wendell Johnson has called "a joint product of our nervous system and certain characteristics of the [thing itself]." "The curtain is blue" becomes a confusion—actually a fusion —of two things: what is inside our heads and what is in the curtain. As Johnson says, "The 'blueness' may be said to be in our head. What the curtain *is* would seem to be something else again. So far as we know there is no 'blueness,' as such, in the curtain; rather there are certain physiochemical phenomena to which, *as we observe them*, we give the name *blue*."

If, however, we are aware of this confusion of the object and how it is seen, we would know that what we are really saying is, "The curtain *seems* blue *to me*," or what Johnson calls *to-me-ness*, just as we might say "The Mayor *seems* honest *to me*," making allowances for people whose definition of honesty is not the same as our own.

The word *is* leads us into still another problem, putting additional limits on our ability to communicate. We give such emphasis to the word *is* that, as we have previously stated, whatever follows the word *is* comes to have a reality all its own. This applies to words such as *good* and *bad*, *right* and *wrong*, *honest* and *dishonest*, and other pairs of words to which we give such emphasis that we tend to ignore the middle areas between the two extremes. This is another problem with absolutes, with ignoring the relative nature of all things. The word *is* further enforces this concept.

> We tend to think in opposites, to feel that what is not good must be bad and that what is not bad must be good.
> —*S. I. Hayakawa*

A thing is either *good* or it's *bad*; it's *pleasant* or *unpleasant*. We tend to disregard the great range of possibilities that do exist between the extremes.

We allow the range of possibilities to disappear especially when we are emotionally charged in one direction or another. These extreme positions are spotted easily when we begin to use phrases like "You're either *for* us or *against* us," or "If you're not part of the *solution*, then you're part of the *problem*." Statements like these destroy the middle ground and obliterate all neutral positions. We lose the benefit of understanding the multiplicity of perspectives when we see things in simpleminded yes or no terms. As S. I. Hayakawa has said, "In the expression, 'We must listen to both sides of every question,' there is an assumption, frequently unexamined, that every question has two sides—and only two sides."

English does, of course, allow us to be less than absolute—we can say things are bad, fair, pretty good, good, or perfect—but because it's harder for us than for the Chinese, we are often lazy about it, and this laziness leads us to much unnecessary daily anguish and even, in some cases, to poor mental health.

Children who are told they *are* "bad" or "stupid" may think badness and stupidity are "real" conditions, a quality that labels them permanently, and absolutely. Such children become limited, not by their own natures, but by the nature of the language and by the limits of the teacher/labeler who forgets about Johnson's *to-me-ness*.

This limit we place on ourselves, and sometimes on other people, is called the *two-valued* orientation, an orientation or relation to the world around us that leaves us balancing one extreme against its opposite while dismissing the advantage of a *multi-valued* orientation, which allows for exploration of the range of possibilities in and solutions to a situation.

The phenomenon of *either/or* thinking, for instance, assumes a two-valued orientation in that there are two sides—and only two sides—to a question. Well, there may be only two sides to the playing cards in a deck, but few situations in our daily experience offer such clearcut choices, though we habitually react as if this were the

case. The mold cast by *either/or* thinking is ever present on a personal level. You're either a good student or a poor student. You either write well or can't write at all. You're either a success or a failure. You're either independent or you're not. You're either pretty or ugly, smart or stupid, my friend or my enemy. Either you love me or you don't! Such reasoning snuffs out a whole range of possibilities, but not just on the personal level. It occurs frequently on the political and historical levels as well.

A typical attitude bearing the stamp of *either/or* thinking was expressed in the words of a man who recently called a midwestern radio station to register his disgust: "The way our liberal Senators, like Mansfield [Montana], Kennedy [Massachusetts], and Eagleton [Missouri], talk, it makes me wonder which side they're on, ours or Russia's." *Either/or* narrows your choices to two, then forces you to choose one. One patriot, fired up by a letter to the editors of the St.

Louis *Post-Dispatch* which had criticized United States foreign policy, wrote back that "for generations my family has supported the stars and stripes on the battlefield and we didn't worry whether the USA was *right or wrong*. I wish to say that I hope to die before I criticize my country on foreign affairs." [Italics mine]

To the Ku Klux Klan you are either anti-Christ or you're not. "Anti-Christ" condemns in a single sweep all peace movements, the United Nations, Jews, and communism. And the Klan's doctrine of white supremacy hardly leaves room for more than an *either/or* mentality. In the same way, the American Nazi party claims that if you hate Nazis then you must love communists. In their search for a "pure" Aryan strain, they would sterilize all Semitic whites, and whites with below normal IQs. All breeding-age blacks would be "encouraged" to consider sterilization; those who wouldn't would be moved to reservations until they could be shipped to Africa. You're pure Aryan or you're not. Thinking individuals should avoid the trap set by *either/or*.

The political arena reaps an ugly harvest of *either/or* close-mindedness. You're either a Republican or a Democrat, a liberal or a conservative. But even worse are the narrowed alternatives offered in times of fear and hysteria. Much of the hysteria in our own country in this century can be summed up in two phrases: "the red menace" and "the yellow peril." Both battle cries—for that is what they each became on more than one occasion—have had tragic consequences, right down to our own time.

In 1919, reaction to "the red menace" culminated in "Palmer's Reign of Terror," raids on suspected communists led by the ambitious Attorney General A. Mitchell Palmer.

In the name of God, Justice, Democracy, and who knows what else, Palmer began a zealous crusade that he hoped would one day make him President. Spectacular raids on suspected radicals in November 1919 were followed by even more spectacular raids in January 1920, when over 4,000 persons were arrested in over thirty cities. State and local governments took their cue and made similar raids with predictably similar results: normal legal procedures were skirted, with deportation of alien radicals as the goal. Few warrants were involved; prisoners were held illegally and not allowed to communicate with family or legal counsel; treatment often was brutally inhumane. Inevitably, false arrests were made, and of course it was the innocent who suffered most. And Palmer—well, he became a national hero. There were no distinguishable degrees of dissent; nonconformity was crucified. You were a radical, revolutionary, bolshevik. Or you weren't.

And in the early 1950s, "McCarthyism" would shamefully recall the dismal insensibility of this earlier period. The Red Scare has never really gone away.

The Yellow Peril, which began in the latter half of the nineteenth century as a mass fear of immigrating Chinese, shifted focus after the Japanese began immigrating in large numbers. At the outbreak of World War II, the new fear—which had been rising steadily—reached a frenzy which resulted in the impoundment in concentration camps of 112,000 persons, "the entire Japanese American population of the three Pacific Coast states of California, Oregon, and Washington," according to Roger Daniels' account, *Concentration Camps U.S.A.* These concentration camps are not to be confused with the Nazi concentration camps of Hitler's Germany, where millions of people were systematically exterminated, but as Roger Daniels has said, "no American can take pride in this sordid episode."

The racism that had been anti-Chinese (they had been considered subhuman) expanded, becoming anti-Japanese in 1890. The discrimination against the Japanese started with the San Francisco laborers, and spread quickly. In 1892 the Mayor of San Francisco declared in a sweeping anti-oriental indictment:

> The Japanese are starting the same tide of immigration which we thought we had checked twenty years ago. . . . The Chinese and Japanese are not bona fide citizens. They are not the stuff of which American citizens can be made.

One Stanford University professor was supposed to have suggested turning guns on those ships that were bringing Japanese in rather than allow them to land.

And so it went, right up to the Japanese attack on Pearl Harbor in December 1941, when things got much worse. It was "Nip," "Mad dogs," and "Yellow Vermin"; the situation became starkly two dimensional. As one newspaper put it, Japs were Japs and whether they were American citizens or not made no difference whatsoever.

Within a matter of months after the attack on Pearl Harbor, all Japanese Americans on the West Coast had been rounded up and the entire nation was locked in the vise-like grip of an *either/or* mentality.

Similarly, there were few alternatives in the single-mindedness of Lenin, the leader of the Russian Revolution. His relentless pursuit of the Revolution so encompassed his being that he frightened even his closest associates (though they had other reason as well to fear him). He once said:

> The people have no need for liberty. Liberty is one of the forms of the bourgeois dictatorship. In a state worthy of the

name there is no liberty. The people want to exercise power, but what on earth would they do if it were given to them? There are three things that have to be done: You must give the earth to the peasants, peace to the soldiers, power to the working class; *and every action which does not directly aim to bring about these three things is non-Marxist and therefore false.* [Italics mine]

You were either Marxist or non-Marxist. Nothing in between. No room to argue. And not many people who stayed alive through those turbulent days did.

But we can hardly maintain a healthy multi-valued orientation and at the same time blame all our troubles on *either/or* thinking. And we certainly can't blame it on the word *is*. It isn't all *is's* fault. Although it is probably true that the pattern of our language has an influence on the pattern of our thinking, we can still control the way we use those patterns. How we use words makes the difference. *Is* isn't something apart, something altogether independent of its user, and we have the responsibility to control our use of it. We can say to the child not, "You are stupid," but instead, "Sticking a bobby pin into the light plug is a stupid thing to do because it will hurt you." Not "You are bad," but "You are being bad right now by hitting your brother." We can't afford the luxury of ignoring all but the extremes.

> The fact remains that many of us, every day, use "is" as if it were some kind of a weapon.
> —Don Fabun

Labelling and stereotyping certainly are instances of the misuse of *is*. Calling someone a *politician* nowadays isn't the kindest of epithets, but it is the caller who should recognize that even a politician is a great many other things, a mother or father, for instance (maybe even a *good* one), or a businessman or businesswoman (maybe even an *honest* one), and possibly a great many other things—all of which become lost in the term *politician*. (It may even be a *fact* that this politician is *decent* and *fair*.) Thus, whenever we claim with great authority, as we often do, that so-and-so *is* such-and-such, we clearly deny all the other is's the person may be. "So-and-so *is* such-and-such," as if there is nothing else to consider, as if nothing else matters.

Finally, our misuse of *is* often leads to that confusion discussed earlier in this book, the failure to separate a word from the thing the word stands for, that problem where in the minds of some the word becomes the thing itself. In November 1973 the school board of Drake, North Dakota (population 600), used the school incinerator at the local high school to rid the town of books containing obscene language. As one resident put it, the words in the books were responsible for undermining the morals of the young. According to the report by the Associated Press, additional "filth" scheduled for burning included works by Hemingway, Faulkner, and Steinbeck.

Thus, it becomes clear that we need to check ourselves, to be aware of the ways in which language limits us and what limits our use of language. As Stuart Chase has noted, the North American Wintu Indians would not say, as we do, that "this is bread"; they would say instead that "we *call* this bread," an accurate and seemingly more sensible way of putting things. Perhaps, it can be argued that this is, in fact, what we mean when we say "this is bread," but it can be argued that most of the time we forget it.

As Don Fabun has said, it seems that many of us use *is* as if it were a weapon. Keep this statement in mind as you consider the following suggestions.

Suggestions

◄§ Select the four or five tallest people in the classroom and have them stand together next to each other. Have the class determine who *is* "tall" and who *is* "short."

◄§ Select some long trips you have taken and discuss how *long* they were. Have any others in the class taken "long" trips? How *long* or *short* was yours by comparison?

◄§ Pick out any slogans you know of that abuse a range of possibilities, and discuss them with the class. Determine the range of alternatives that actually exist. Discuss, for instance, the declaration that "Not to decide is to decide," or "You're either for us or against us." (In historian Dumas Malone's *Jefferson and the Ordeal of Liberty*, he reminds us that this last expression is nearly as old as the country itself. During the political feud that raged between the Federalist and Republican parties in 1798 and beyond, the slogan of the *Gazette of the United States* (a leading paper for the Federalists) declared, "He that is not for us, is against us." This same paper also warned a few months later that to write in favor of the government showed patriotism, to write against it was sedition.)

◄§ Read carefully the following statement about the era of the American Revolution made years later (1816) by Thomas Jefferson in a letter to a friend:

> In truth, the abuses of monarchy had so much filled all the space of political contemplation that we •imagined everything republican which was not monarchy. We had not yet penetrated to the mother principle, that "governments are republican only in proportion as they embody the will of the people and execute it."

Was Jefferson guilty of *either/or* thinking during that frenzied period— or wasn't he? Explain your answer.

◄§ Discuss the statement that "emotionally, a person is either strong or weak." Are there more than just the two categories, *strong* and *weak?* Is it possible for a person to be both, that is emotionally strong in dealing with one problem, emotionally weak in dealing with another problem? Is it possible to be strong at one moment and weak at another moment in dealing with the same problem? Do *strong* and *weak* exist apart from our perception of them? Discuss these questions as they apply to the statements earlier, such as "Either you love me or you don't!" Discuss other similar statements. Take a situation in your life that reflects the difficulty raised here and write about it *in your journal*. Discuss this statement of the Chinese poet Seng T'san: "The struggle between 'for' and 'against' is the mind's worst disease."

⋙ *In your journal*, record a personal experience in which a two-valued orientation prevailed over a more useful and sensible multi-valued orientation. Describe and discuss with the class how the situation might have been different if the person or persons involved had used the multi-valued approach. Do the same using an example from politics or history, past or present.

⋙ Classify yourself in as many categories as you can think of. How many different things are you? Think about the community, city, state, and country you live in. Are you a tennis enthusiast? A fishing enthusiast? Are you a "bookworm"? An athlete? Are you religious? Do you attend church regularly? Are you a man? Woman? Mother? Uncle? Cousin? Think about what you do during the course of a day in addition to attending college. Classify yourself accordingly. Would you object to being classified by the word *is* as one of these things and one thing only? Explain.

5 Language and Thought: Persuasion and Propaganda

Words, as we have pointed out earlier, do not exist independent of the user or receiver. To paraphrase Shakespeare, "The fault, dear Brutus, is not in our words,/ But in ourselves. . . ." Words do not contain atoms of meaning or electrons of emotional impact; we give them their meaning and impact as we send and receive them. And we receive them almost constantly.

Modern technology has intensified the relentless pounding each of us absorbs nearly every day, from newspapers, magazines, radio, television, billboards, and other people. As former Madison Avenue advertising man Samm Sinclair Baker describes it:

> You bask on a sunny beach enjoying yourself, until you look up and see a skywriting plane belching out: YOU LOOK BURNED—COOL IT WITH NOXEMA. Perhaps the pen you use to write a love letter proclaims itself as a gift of the People's Bank for Savings. The last strains of soothing music from your bedside radio are interrupted by ratcheting jingles: 'Mr. Clean . . . Mr. Clean . . . Mr. Clean . . .'

And even before the advent of television, sociologist David Riesman could write in 1950 that "[t]he child begins to be bombarded by radio and comics from the moment he can listen and just barely read." More recently Nicholas Johnson, former head of the Federal Communication Commission, gathered these statistics about television:

> There are 60 million homes in the United States and over 95 percent of them are equipped with a television set. (More than 25 percent have two or more sets.) In the average home the television is turned on some five hours forty-five minutes a day. The average male viewer, between his second and sixty-fifth year, will watch television for over 3,000 entire days—roughly nine full years of his life. During the average weekday winter

evening nearly half of the American people are to be found silently seated with fixed gaze upon a phosphorescent screen.

By now we are so steeped in our television that it is often difficult to distinguish the real from the unreal. "It was unbelievable," remarked a startled witness to a bank holdup on a New York City street. "Here was this man waving a gun, and I kept looking around to see where the movie cameras were." As if to emphasize the point, several months later in May 1974, a Los Angeles driver saw some men armed with machine guns backing out of a bank entrance. To avoid being shot, she ducked under the dashboard, lost control of the car, and struck stunt men and movie extras involved in filming a robbery scene. Baker states that "[f]or many families who live inside the TV box, the most real thing in life becomes the plainly unreal world of television." The barrage is ceaseless, and we have become very susceptible to the verbal assaults of persuasion and propaganda.

Both persuasion and propaganda deal with what Walter Lippmann has called, "the effort to alter the picture to which men respond. . . ." The word *persuasion* usually refers to one person's or one group's attempt to direct or redirect the thoughts or actions of another person or group. The word *propaganda* involves much the same attempt, though it usually has a less favorable connotation than does persuasion because propaganda has so often been associated with appeals made by "bad" people. In other words, when we do it to them, it's persuasion; when they do it to us, it's propaganda. But neither persuasion nor propaganda by itself is necessarily good or evil: it is the motives, the desired ends, of the persons or groups in their attempts to persuade that make the difference.

Hitler's motives were certainly sinister, and he deftly wove fear and prejudice into his holocaustic pattern. He knew what the crowd wanted to hear and he gave it to them, making him a master of *ad populum* (appeal to the crowd) persuasion. As Robert Payne explains in *The Life and Death of Adolf Hitler*:

> Deeper than Hitler's hatred of the Jews was the knowledge that they could be used for his own ambitions, his own cold-blooded purposes. When he inveighed against them in his speeches, he noted the sudden roar of approval from the embittered veterans who wanted someone to blame for Germany's defeat [in World War I] and their own hopeless poverty. Leaderless, they were only too willing to be led.

Still, not all propaganda or persuasion is evil, despite general contempt for the word propaganda. We can hardly attribute sinister motives to Woodsy Owl or to a more famous predecessor, Smokey

> Propaganda is expression of opinion or action by individuals or groups deliberately designed to influence opinions or actions of other individuals or groups. . . .
> —Clyde Miller

Courtesy, U.S. Department of Agriculture

Bear, who continues to receive so much fan mail that the United States Post Office has given Smokey a separate zip code number. But their pleas, their attempts to persuade, are propaganda, just as our own pleas so often are, and we should recognize that we are as likely to propagandize as Woodsy, or Smokey, or Adolf Hitler. For we are not always on the receiving end.

Who, after all, has not tried to change or channel another person's thinking? Who has not been a propagandist, the person who attempts to convert others to accept a particular view by whatever persuasive means that can be mustered?

As Daniel Callahan has suggested in his book *Abortion: Law, Choice, and Morality*, "[s]ince it is true in a democratic society that the group which screams the loudest and longest is liable to triumph, it is not, as tactics go, a bad one." And some people do scream. On the controversial issue of the Equal Rights Amendment for women, *Newsweek* Magazine, in January 1973, reported on some of the legislators of one state who "scaled oratorical heights" in denouncing it:

'I see the darkness of increasing alcoholism and suicide,' one thundered. Others predicted 'pimps and prostitutes everywhere,' with armies of 'homosexuals, bisexuals and other deviators' coming out of the closets. There was a curious fear that ERA would ban sex distinctions in public toilets and a dark reminiscence of 'the Russian Army with men and women . . . squatting over open latrines.'

As journalist H. L. Mencken insisted earlier in this century: "All talk of winning the people by appealing to their intelligence . . . is so much moonshine."

In addition to these appeals to our emotions, persuasion and propaganda are aided by whatever personal appeal the persuader or propagandist has. Such personal appeal is variously known as charm, tact, diplomacy, or charisma. It's not a simple matter of getting the correct spray can; those people who possess charisma or tact usually know how to use it. Any public figure, politician or movie star, knows how valuable a commodity it is. Those blessed with it seldom let it go to waste.

Drawing by Ed Fisher; copyright © 1969 The New Yorker Magazine, Inc.

Squeezed in between the motives of the persuader and the prejudices of the audience is, of course, the message itself. It is something carefully considered by the shrewd propagandist who has probably already spent a good deal of time taking stock of his or her own appeal, and of the emotions and prejudices of the person or group that he or she is trying to persuade. The message will take shape, reflecting considerations of these two factors, as well as of the content of the message.

For the propagandist, the audience becomes the target; the message, something to be manipulated; the purpose, to get others to think a certain thought or act a certain way. Thus, propaganda and persuasion are neither fair nor unfair; they are the ways in which one person influences another to gain desired ends—whether good or bad.

Again, there is nothing inherently wrong with attempts to persuade. But as Clyde Miller, founder in 1937 of the Institute for Propaganda Analysis, points out, "the intelligent citizen does not want to be 'used' in the attainment of ends he may later consider 'bad.' He does not want to be duped, even in a 'good' cause." So whenever only *some* of the facts are given, or someone cries "communist" or "fascist" we had better be awake. Smokey the Bear and Woodsy Owl, for all their attempts to persuade, never withheld information or worked for destructive ends. But there are those who will, and we had better be alert.

Something we need to be keenly aware of is the use of language which, of course, plays a major role in the persuader's appeal to the emotions of the audience. The choice of words will color what is being said. The Equal Rights Amendment, for example, remains a hotly contested issue, a fact reflected in the language surrounding it.

Phyllis Schlafly, a housewife, stands against its passage and has crisscrossed the country saying so. She has worked to defeat the amendment, which needs to be ratified by thirty-eight State Legislatures in order to become the twenty-sixth amendment to the United States Constitution. "The Equal Rights Amendment is a terminal case. The only question remaining is whether its sponsors will let it die peacefully, and with dignity, or whether they will engage in massive bloodletting in a vain attempt to save their offspring." Such words and phrases as "terminal case," "die," "dignity," and "massive bloodletting," are all charged words. They constitute an attempt to have us react a certain way, not to the merits (or lack of them) of the Equal Rights Amendment, but to see the situation precisely as the speaker wishes us to see it.

On the other side of the issue, but with similar use of language, history professor Dr. Jacqueline St. John, has said, "Let us face the harsh truth—we are the 'silenced majority'! Any woman who is so foolish as to believe that 'we have come a long way, baby' is living in a child's temporary paradise—the chocolate factory, also inhabited by the tooth fairy, Tinkerbell and the Easter Bunny." Just as in the preceding case, the charged language—"the harsh truth," "the silenced majority," "a child's temporary paradise," "the chocolate factory," and so on—attempts to align our thoughts with those of the speaker.

These are examples of the use of what Daniel Callahan has called "language designed to change laws [and] incite emotions," an ever-present phenomenon on all sides of an issue. To suspect the opposition of employing charged language and emotional appeals, while remaining convinced that our allies represent paragons of coolheaded

Except for downright dangerous indifference to accurate information (say the information on labels in a druggist's shop), we tend to believe what we want to believe.
—*Weller Embler*

reason, is itself a trap. It is difficult enough to separate our emotional attachment from an issue; it is impossible to separate our emotions from the reality we "see."

This very point is raised in *Alistair Cooke's America,* Cooke's penetrating account of the history of the United States. In recounting the famous historical incident which follows, Cooke makes an interesting connection between individual passion and the broad scope of history.

> . . . it takes only so much continuous taunting to provoke a reaction out of all proportion to the original prod. Parliament ought to have been warned, but was not, by a small episode of insurrection that happened in Boston, on a snowy March day in 1770, outside the Customs House, the port of entry for British indignities and by now the detested symbol of Parliament's authority. It was guarded on that day by a single sentry. There is a great variety of versions of what happened: some toughs attacked the sentry, or he was showing off his swordsmanship and nipped a bystander in the arm, or somebody was beaten up. At any rate, a small crowd gathered and started to jeer at the sentry and throw stones and slivers of ice. He shouted for help, and more soldiers came running and lined up in formation to guard him and the Customs House. At some point the crowd grew scared, or bold, and one of the soldiers was clubbed and kicked to the ground. As he tried to get up, he slipped on the ice and his musket went off. So far that is what we should call the Establishment story. It is not disputed that after the first shot, the crowd charged and some of the soldiers panicked and fired. *What happened next—as in most riots with political overtones—depends on the passion and the prejudice of whichever side you were on when you first heard about it. That, too, is history—not what happened, but what people convinced themselves must have happened.* [Italics mine]

Suggestions

◄§   In 1962 Rachel Carson wrote *Silent Spring,* a book that warned that the use of chemicals in an effort to kill certain insects was, in turn, likely to kill all forms of life if not used wisely. Her book created a "national quarrel" with the chemical industry and its spokesman, Dr. Robert White-Stevens. In 1963 CBS televised an hour special on the controversy.* Here, in part, is what Rachel Carson and Robert White-Stevens had to say:

CARSON: Chemicals are the sinister and little recognized
               partners of radiation in changing the very na-

---

* © 1974 Columbia Broadcasting System, Inc. All Rights Reserved. Excerpt of transcript reproduced from CBS REPORTS, "The Silent Spring of Rachel Carson," broadcast over the CBS Television Network on April 2, 1963.

ture of the world, the very nature of its life. Since the mid 1940s over 200 basic chemicals have been created for use in killing insects, weeds, rodents, and other organisms, described in the modern vernacular as "pests" and they are sold under several thousand different brand names. These sprays, dusters, and aerosols are now applied almost universally to farms, gardens, forests, and homes. Nonselective chemicals that have the power to kill every insect—the good and the bad—to still the song of birds, the leaping of fish in the streams, to coat the leaves with a deadly film, and to linger on in soil. All this where the intended target may be only a few weeds or insects.

Can anyone believe it is possible to lay down such a barrage of poisons on the surface of the earth without making it unfit for all life? They should not be called "insecticides" but "biocides."

WHITE-STEVENS: The major claims in Miss Rachel Carson's book *The Silent Spring* are gross distortions of the actual facts, completely unsupported by scientific experimental evidence and general practical experience in the field. Her suggestion that pesticides are, in fact, biocides destroying all life is obviously absurd in light of the fact that without selective biological activity these compounds would be completely useless. The real threat, then, to the survival of man is not chemical but biological in the shape of hordes of insects that can denude our forests, sweep over crop lands, ravage our food supply, and leave in their wake a train of destitution and hunger, conveying to an undernourished population the major diseases and scourges of mankind. If man were to faithfully follow the teaching of Miss Carson, we would return to the Dark Ages and the insects and diseases and vermin would once again inherit the earth.

Study the two points of view presented here on the use of chemicals to kill insects. Are the appeals emotional? If so, in what ways? What particular words or phrases are used to invoke sympathy? (Be careful that your own sympathies with one view or the other do not blind you to the emotional appeal that may exist in one or both.) Is the appeal to emotion *good* or *bad*, *fair* or *unfair*? Explain your answer.

◄§ What do you mean by *good* and *bad*, *fair* and *unfair*"?

∾   Attend a trial and take notes on how language is used by the lawyers (who are ordinarily advocates and hence subjective) and by the judge (who is by definition objective and dispassionate). Analyze the trial in terms of what you know about the use of language to persuade and manipulate.

∾   Find examples of different approaches to the same controversial issue—opinion on abortion, amnesty, and so on. Bring in the newspaper articles, editorials, or speeches and the like. Discuss the use of any language "designed to change laws or to incite emotions. . . ." Discuss Daniel Callahan's statement that "a plurality of value systems in a society not only assures a conflict of values in that society, and thus a situation of disagreement, it also seems to assure that each group within a society will hold on all the more tenaciously to its own viewpoint. . . ."

∾   Discuss historical incidents, or personal experiences, or imaginary situations which would correspond to Cooke's evaluation as it is explained in the italicized portion. Determine with the help of the class how much a part personal prejudices and emotions played or would have played.

∾   Is it possible to use language without trying to persuade? (The correct answer is no.) Discuss.

Whenever persuasion and propaganda are evident factors, whenever passion and prejudice create a necessary connection between words and emotions, the interaction of language and thought leads to numerous instances of deflected and distorted reasoning. In such instances, the unwary become the prey, quick to consider wholly irrelevant matters, or worse, to reach unwarranted conclusions.

Many such examples of breakdowns in the reasoning process are given below, and where it is possible traditional terminology has been attached to them, as it was earlier in the case of Hitler's appeal to the crowd (*ad populum*). But terminology is not the major concern; not every example will neatly fit a single term, and more than one term may fit a single example.

There are more important questions:

> Do we see cause and effect relationships where none exist?
> Is anything left out of the reasoning process?
> What specific claims are made?
> Is the central question avoided altogether, whether intentionally or not?
> Is any particular appeal made? What effect does it have?
> Is there any attempt to purposely mislead? Are we given all the facts?
> What attempts are made to manipulate certain words and phrases to suit a purpose?

Each of these more basic and essential considerations will now be discussed in turn.

Do we see cause and effect relationships where none exist?

On August 19, 1973, twenty-six-year-old Herbert Mullin was convicted in Santa Cruz, California, of the murder of ten people. Admitting the murders, Mullin insisted that the human "sacrifices" were necessary to prevent an earthquake from destroying the state. His lawyer entered a plea of "innocent," insisting that Mullin, in the grip of LSD-induced insanity, had murdered a young couple, a woman and her two young sons, four teenagers and others. Within hours of the jury's verdict of "guilty," earth tremors hit the southern California area and local police departments were deluged with frightened callers, some of whom insisted that the tremors were punishment for sentencing Mullin.

People who insist on a cause and effect relationship where none exists are assuming that one event causes a second event that follows it in time. Insisting on such a relationship is formally known by the Latin term *post hoc, ergo propter hoc,* meaning literally *"after this, therefore because of this."* In other words, when one event follows another event, the second event is thought to be caused by the first. Some people establish a cause and effect relationship in their minds (as have the persons who saw the earth tremors as a result of the jury's verdict of guilty) when in reality no such relationship exists.

Faulty cause and effect reasoning is also evident in superstitions. If we do a certain thing a certain way, we can make something else happen. Professional athletes, for example, are notorious for their superstitious behavior. Bob Burnes, Sports Editor for the St. Louis *Globe–Democrat,* has noted that most superstitions start as a result of something good happening after the first time the athlete does something. Enos Slaughter, a 1940s star for the St. Louis baseball Cardinals, while at bat once stepped out of the batter's box, took the wad of gum he had been chewing, struck it on the button of his cap, stepped back into the batter's box and slammed a home run. For the rest of his baseball career, whenever he was at bat, he invariably took a wad of gum from his mouth and stuck it on the button of his cap. Other baseball players, Burnes notes, touch third base or first on their way out to the outfield or on their way in to the dugout; pitchers carefully avoid stepping on the foul line going to or returning from the mound. Hockey star Stan Mikita of the Chicago Blackhawks has to be the last skater onto the ice before a game and once on the ice goes through a series of weird leg bending exercises. Burnes then recounts the strangest superstition he has ever known about, involving basketball player Richie Guerin when he was with the St. Louis (now the Atlanta) Hawks. "Just before a game one night," tells Burnes, "he had an urgent need to visit the men's room. He ducked out just before the national anthem. By the time he returned, the game had started and the Hawks had scored three quick baskets. For a couple of years, he disappeared up the runway just before the start of every game, whether there was an urgency or not."

The string of such stories is probably nearly as long as the list of athletes; and superstition, as most of us will admit, is not confined to professional athletes. Whenever superstition is involved, if we go through certain rituals, do a certain thing a certain way, so the reasoning goes, something good will surely follow or something bad will be avoided.

Closely related to superstitions are omens. Just how seriously they can be taken is revealed in the following incident recounted by Robert K. Massie in *Nicholas and Alexandra*, the biography of the last Russian Tsar and Tsaritsa whose fates were sealed with the rise of Lenin and the coming of the Russian Revolution in 1917. The incident occurred during the five hour coronation of Tsar Nicholas and Tsaritsa Alexandra in May 1896:

> While everyone else remained standing, Nicholas alone dropped to his knees to pray for Russia and her people. After being anointed with Holy Oil, Nicholas swore his oath to rule the empire and preserve autocracy as Emperor and Autocrat of all the Russias. Then, for the first time and only time in his life, the Tsar entered the sanctuary to receive the sacrament as a priest of the church. As Nicholas walked up the altar steps, the heavy chain of the Order of St. Andrew slipped from his shoulders and fell to the floor. It happened so quickly that no one noticed except those standing close to the Tsar. Later, lest it be taken as an omen, all these were sworn to secrecy.

(Little more than twenty years later, Nicholas and his family were murdered—and with them, Imperial Russia. We will leave it to the advocates of *post hoc* reasoning to make their own case.)

Darrell Huff, in a chapter titled "Post Hoc Rides Again," from his book *How to Lie with Statistics*, cites this example of people who have assumed that event A caused event B just because B occurred after A. A conviction held among the people of the New Hebrides was that body lice produced good health.

> Observation over the centuries had taught them that people in good health usually had lice and sick people very often did not. The observation itself was accurate and sound, as observations made informally over the years surprisingly often are. Not much can be said for the conclusion to which these primitive

people came from their evidence: Lice make a man healthy. Everybody should have them. . . . More sophisticated observers finally got things straightened out in the New Hebrides. As it turned out, almost everybody in those circles had lice most of the time. It was, you might say, the normal condition of man. When, however, anyone took a fever (quite possibly carried to him by those same lice) and his body became too hot for comfortable habitation, the lice left. There you have cause and effect altogether confusingly distorted, reversed, and intermingled.

Suggestions

~§   Describe an incident in which you or someone you know of saw a cause and effect relationship where none existed. Find an example in the media of a cause and effect relationship that has no basis in fact. Describe it *in your journal* and discuss it with the class.

~§   What superstitions do you have? What about those of your family and friends? Discuss the reasoning behind those superstitions. To what degree do your friends or members of your family believe in omens? What is the reasoning behind those beliefs?

Is anything left out of the reasoning process?

In *Paper Lion*, George Plimpton recalls a story about Jack Benny, for decades one of America's foremost comedy stars—and one of its worst violinists. "Jack Benny used to say that when he stood on the stage in white tie and tails for his violin concerts and raised his bow to begin his routine—scraping through [his theme song] 'Love in Bloom'—that he *felt* like a great violinist. He reasoned that, if he wasn't a great violinist, what was he doing dressed in tails, and about to play before a large audience?"

Despite the fact that Benny at times looked the part and even felt the part, he was at all times still a lousy violinist. The reasoning he used, known as *arguing in a circle*, states that "something is this (or that) because it is this (or that)." In other words, "x is true because x is true." Statements such as "We should be loyal to our country because it is the patriotic thing to do" don't do a very good job of explaining why we should be loyal. The statement really says that we should be loyal because we should be loyal, which doesn't seem to get us very far. With this method of reasoning, we end up about where we started.

Sometimes vital statistics—left out or forgotten—leave a gap in the reasoning process. As Darrell Huff warns in *How to Lie with Statistics*, "you can use accident statistics to scare yourself to death in connection with any kind of transportation . . . *if you fail to note how poorly attached the figures are.*" [Italics mine] As an example, Huff points out that you can show that driving in clear weather is more dangerous than driving in foggy weather. The fact that there is a great deal more clear than foggy weather seems to be forgotten. Similarly, he cites how people can draw the conclusion that modern airplanes are more dangerous than those used in 1910, since more people are killed now than they were then. One comes to this absurd conclusion by failing to attach today's enormously increased number of flights and thousands more passengers. It does *not* follow, then, that air travel is more dangerous now than in 1910—at least not based on the information given.

In still another way, drawing unjustified conclusions may short circuit the reasoning process. Generalizations are the most common example of this, so common, in fact, that we need to examine what generalizations are and answer some questions about them, in an effort to clear up some generalizations about generalizations.

First, what is a generalization? In the *Art of Making Sense*, Lionel Ruby defines a generalization as "a statement that *goes beyond* what is actually observed, to a rule or law covering both the observed cases and those that have not as yet been observed." For example, if we assume on the basis of those few southern Californians who connected Mullin's prophecy with the earth tremors that all Californians are *post hoc* thinkers, then we are drawing a conclusion, making a generalization, on the basis of extremely limited evidence. This generalization becomes a matter of going beyond generalizing, to *jumping to conclusions*.

Second, are *all* generalizations false? No. Some are, some aren't. When we generalize, then, we assume a lot on the basis of a little. Some conclusions, however, are reasonable and dependable; some are not. No neat and absolute line divides one from the other. Like classification, generalization can be extremely useful in thought and communication. But there are dangers: just as classification may lead to stereotyping, generalization may lead to a hasty conclusion, such as the one Sally reaches on her first visit to the library.

Third, are *all* generalizations useless? Again, no. Proverbs, for instance, which are part of all human cultures, are generalizations, and though they often contradict one another ("absence makes the heart grow fonder," but "out of sight, out of mind"), they are there for those who wish to use them and they do, after all, offer a choice.

Some generalizations, as we have pointed out, are useful: others not only are not, they may even be harmful. When we assume something, draw a conclusion about what we hear or see, we can often be incorrect, as was the woman described in this letter to Ann Landers:

Dear Ann Landers:

People used to whisper about homosexuality. Now they are hollering about it. Will you please do the world a favor and tell

them not to jump to conclusions? What appears at a glance to be deviant behavior just might be a normal display of affection.

Last weekend a close friend and I went out for a cocktail. I'd had a bad day and, as luck would have it, two men joined us— or rather, joined her, I was in a depressed mood and excused myself to go to the ladies' room. For some mysterious reason I began to cry. My friend came in shortly after and when she saw me, she became upset and asked if I was angry with her. I told her my depression had nothing to do with her and that I loved her like a sister. She put her arms around me and said, "I love you, too."

At that very moment a woman came in. In a voice filled with disgust she snapped, "I wish you Gay Libbers would stay in your own homes." We were speechless.

Please inform your readers that physical contact doesn't necessarily carry a sexual connotation. A hug can be a reassuring and comforting gesture. In fact, I felt closer to the whole human race when my friend embraced me, and believe me, I'm as normal as they come.

I love you, too, Ann, for letting me get this off my chest.

—*Straight in Corpus Christi*

As the writer of this letter indicates, jumping to conclusions should be avoided. Being careless in drawing conclusions interferes with our ability to arrive at useful generalizations and greatly hinders meaningful communication.

Suggestions

◄§   In each of the examples of gaps in the reasoning process discussed in this section, determine how harmful or harmless, fair or unfair, each is.

◄§   Discuss the reasoning (or lack of it) used by the school superintendent who refused a request to include a foreign language in the curriculum. His reason: if English was good enough for Jesus, then surely it was good enough for those making the request.

◄§   Read the following letter:

To the Editors:
   One solution to the gasoline shortage would be to raise the driver's license age limit to 18 years old. We have approximately 15,000,000 students in high schools across the country. Of this number I suspect 9,000,000 have some type of car or motorcycle using gasoline at the rate of about 30,000,000 gallons per day. Such a limit could have other benefits, such as: better grades, fewer accidents and deaths, reduced drug abuse, fewer unwed teen-age mothers, worried parents, court cases for our overworked judges, lessened family debt and insurance costs, and more responsible teenagers.
   This much savings in gasoline could keep 15,000 traveling salesmen averaging 30,000 miles per year in fuel. These people add to the great economy of this country, whereas the 15, 16, and 17 year old driver adds very little to the GNP.

The author of this letter assumes that 15-, 16-, and 17-year-olds deprived of their automobiles will benefit by making better grades, having fewer accidents, reducing their drug intake, having fewer illegitimate babies, and so on. Discuss the conclusions drawn here by the writer of the letter. How logical is each? Which conclusions do you agree with? Which do you disagree with? Explain your answers.

◄§   Distinguish between valid generalizations and hasty conclusions. Make a list of generalizations, some valid, some not. Discuss particular situations in which you or someone you know drew valid generalizations. Discuss particular situations in which you or someone you know drew unwarranted, hasty conclusions.

◄§   Recall proverbs that you know. What purpose do they serve? Are any contradictory? Is the fact that some of them are contradictory harmful? Explain. How much stock do you and the people you know put in them?

What specific claims are made?
Claims are made in many ways. Think for a moment about the

wife (in her typically stereotyped role) who, if she will simply have enough sense to serve her husband the correct brand of coffee, can remove the only obstacle in the way of an otherwise thoroughly blissful marriage. Similarly, think about the man who by using the right cologne can become a legend "in his own time." It's simple enough, as cut and dried as an equation:

"X" Cologne → applied to the face = a living legend

Thus, we have the "good life" reduced to a formula that establishes nothing but claims a great deal.

Other claims may involve more than pushing a product. Call someone a name, attach a label to him or her, and we are relieved of the responsibility of finding out who the individual really is and what he or she has to say on an issue. Not unlike stereotyping, *name calling* and labeling disregard all the other aspects of an individual's personality—all except the label attached, and somehow we never seem to find out whether it is an accurate one or not. Such inaccuracy, Robert Goldston tells us in *The Russian Revolution*, led Karl Marx to declare once that "whatever else [Marx] was, he was certainly not a Marxist!"

This does not mean, however, that every instance of attaching a name or label is either inaccurate or uncomplimentary. As Lionel Ruby has advised in *The Art of Making Sense*, "it is not improper to characterize a man as a communist or a fascist when these words are adequately defined and there is proof that these statements are true. When persons are called communists or fascists merely because they espouse views that are more liberal or less liberal than our own, however, we exhibit intellectual irresponsibility."

A classic instance of such "intellectual irresponsibility" occurred in the political arena of this country during the early 1950s. The Chinese communist takeover of Mainland China in 1949 was the major shaping force of United States foreign policy in the Far East. It still is. The Vietnam war was an outgrowth of that policy. In journalist David Halberstam's penetrating account of how we became embroiled in Vietnam, he discusses what came to be known as "McCarthyism." (The term itself soon became a label.) How casually it all began and how tragic it all became are recounted in Halberstam's *The Best and the Brightest*, from which the following is taken:

> On February 9, 1950, McCarthy flew into Wheeling, West Virginia, where he made the first of his major Red-baiting Communist-conspiracy charges: "While I cannot take the time to name all the men in the State Department who have been named as members of the Communist party and members of a

There are some people who, intellectually at least, never seem to rise above or go beyond the mere naming of things, which for them constitutes knowledge, even truth.
—Weller Embler

spy ring, I have here in my hand a list of two hundred and five that were known to the Secretary of State as being members of the Communist party and who, nevertheless, are still working and shaping policy in the State Department. . . .

. . . Around the country he flew, reckless and audacious, stopping long enough to make a new charge, to exhibit a new list, a good newsworthy press conference at the airport, hail-fellow well met with the reporters, and then on to the next stop, the emptiness of the charge never catching up with him . . . It was like a circus; he was always on the move, his figures varied, his work was erratic and sloppy, he seemed to have no genuine interest in any true nature of security. It sometimes seemed as if he too were surprised by the whole thing, how easy it was, how little resistance he met, and so he hurtled forward to newer, larger charges. But if they did not actually stick, and they did not, his charges had an equally damaging effect; they poisoned. Where there was smoke, there must be fire. He wouldn't be saying those things unless there was something to it. And so the contamination remained after the facts, or lack of them, evaporated; long after the specifics had faded into obscurity, the stain remained. . . . The legacy of it all was poison.

Suggestions

‽ Is *name calling* in itself an instance of labeling or calling names? Explain.

‽ In the letter to Ann Landers written by "Straight in Corpus Christi," is there an instance of labeling? Explain.

‽ Relate an incident in which a claim is made. Recount the incident *in your journal* and discuss it with the class. Who or what was involved? What was the result? Determine if the claim was fair or unfair, harmful or harmless.

Is the central question avoided altogether, whether intentionally or not?

A clear instance of avoiding the question occurs in an informative pamphlet distributed by an anti-abortion group in the Midwest. Questions are asked and, for the most part, the answers are given— but not always: **Q.** "What if the[pregnant]mother threatens suicide?" **A.** "Suicide among pregnant women is almost unknown. In Minnesota [for example], in a 15-year period, there were only 14 maternal suicides. Eleven occurred after delivery. None were illegitimately pregnant. All were psychotic."

Interesting and informative facts. But does it answer the question? Does it tell us what to do if the mother threatens suicide?

Another way of avoiding the central issue is simply to assume (intentionally or not) that what is still in question is already true. This is known as *begging the question*. When Theodore Roosevelt said that "[t]his great continent could not have been kept as nothing but a game preserve for squalid savages," he assumed without debate that Indian Americans were squalid savages. When Hitler and the Nazis spoke about the "Jewish problem," they *assumed* that there was such a thing as a Jewish problem. The same assumption is apparently made by people in this country who speak of the "Negro problem" or the "Indian problem." Think about the hidden assumption lurking in the shadows of such statements as "We have to do something to solve the Negro problem."

More deliberate are those attempts to divert our attention from the issues which direct an attack on the personal character of the individual, a tactic known as *ad hominem*. Whether the person's churchgoing or child beating has any connection with the issues is of no importance. Only the attack itself begins to matter.

The late Utah Senator Arthur V. Watkins served in Congress from 1947 to 1959, and in 1954 he presided over the Special Committee looking into possible censure charges against Senator Joseph McCarthy of Wisconsin, whose tragic scenario had been played out during the early 1950s. Rather than answer the charges set forth by the Committee and the Congress (both of which eventually did in effect censure him), McCarthy—never to be caught on the defensive—launched an attack charging that Watkins was "cowardly" and "stupid," and that the Committee he headed was the "unwitting handmaiden of the Communist party."

If the attack shifts attention from the issue to the individual, then it has accomplished its goal. In some areas, courtrooms for instance, such arguments are an accepted and essential part of the trappings, widely used by lawyers in attempts to discredit witnesses who may have offered damaging evidence against their clients. When there is no other way to refute the testimony of a victim or witness, an attack on the character and background of that witness can be the lawyers' (and their clients') best friend.

But the general tactic of distraction is not confined to the courtroom, and may shift from attacking someone personally to attacking another issue (called the *red herring*), thereby diverting attention from the central issue. In December of 1973 the National Observer held a reader plebiscite on whether President Nixon should stay on the job or resign. Many voters added letters to their ballots.

One such letter provides an example of the *red herring* fallacy. The letter asked what the hell the Democrats were trying to do since they were responsible for the Watergate mess in the first place. And since the Democrats had started inflation—the letter proclaimed—and had started the segregation issue, and had started all our wars, it was clear that now they were trying to start a civil war.

Still another person's letter began with the reminder that evangelist Billy Graham had warned in 1965 that the communists intended to control the world by 1975 and that Americans were blind in failing to detect what was really happening behind the scenes.

What the Democrats or Republicans were responsible for historically, and what Billy Graham had said in 1965 about what the communists would do by 1975, hardly speak to the point of whether or not a president should resign.

Suggestions

⋅§ Recount instances—personal or otherwise—in which the central question was avoided. What were the circumstances? In what way was the central issue or question avoided? Who avoided the issue? Someone else? You? Was it intentional? Deceitful? Vicious? Harmful? Fair? Comforting? Explain.

⋅§ In the Letter to the Editors, is there a hidden assumption in the final sentence ("These people [salesmen] add to the great economy of this country, whereas the 15, 16, and 17 year old driver adds very little to the GNP")? Explain.

Is any particular appeal made? What effect does it have?

During the first phase of the Senate Watergate hearings in July 1973, Chairman Sam Ervin engaged in the following heated exchange with Florida's Senator Edward Gurney, also on the committee, who had challenged the severity of Ervin's questioning of former President Nixon's Secretary of the Treasury, Maurice Stans:

GURNEY: The American public, I don't think, understands how these committee hearings are conducted.

. . . and I don't want them to get the impression that the questioning of any Senator here has found favor by other Senators. And I for one have not appreciated the harassment of this witness [Stans] by the Chairman [Ervin] in the questioning that has just finished. I think this Senate Committee ought to act in fairness.

ERVIN: Well, I have not questioned the veracity [Ervin had mistakenly thought that Gurney had said "veracity" instead of "harassment"] of the witness. I have asked the witness to find out what the truth is.

GURNEY: I didn't use the word "veracity." I used the word "harassment."

ERVIN: [Again does not hear the word "Harassment" in the noisy Hearing Room and turns to an aide to find out what word Gurney had used.] What?

ERVIN'S AIDE: "Harassment."

ERVIN: "Harassment?"

GURNEY: "Harassment. H-A-R-A-S-S-M-E-N-T."
[Laughter in the Hearing Room]

ERVIN: Well, I'm sorry that my distinguished friend from Florida does not approve of my method of examing the witness. I'm an old country lawyer, and I don't know the finer ways to do it. I just have to do it my way.
[Applause in the Hearing Room]

This "old country lawyer," it should be noted, who doesn't know "the finer ways," attended the University of North Carolina and the Harvard Law School, was a county judge in 1935, and a judge of the North Carolina Superior Court by 1937; he became a member of the North Carolina Supreme Court in 1948, and finally became a member of the United States Senate in 1954.

So he's been around—at least enough to know how effective the often used *plain folks* appeal can be. And as an old country schoolteacher, Lyndon B. Johnson, put it: "Whenever I hear someone say 'I'm just an old country lawyer,' the first thing I reach for is my wallet to make sure it's still there."

And if Senator Ervin needed historical precedent for such an appeal, he had it. In *Alistair Cooke's America*, Cooke relates the appeal used by one of the rabble-rousing heroes of the American Revolution, the aristocratic Samuel Adams: "Tough, tender, and wily, he used to rough up his appearance and wear threadbare clothes on public occasions to show his bond with the common people."

Product endorsements are another example of appeal by association. In September 1973, in one of the most highly publicized tennis matches in the history of the game, middle-aged Bobby Riggs ("the nation's Number One-seeded male chauvinist") squared off against the nation's reigning female tennis player, Billie Jean King. The game itself seemed strictly secondary as the advertising agencies quickly smothered both stars as soon as the contest caught on as this century's decisive battle of the sexes. "We're being approached by manufacturers of everything from vitamins to socks," claimed the talent agency that handled Riggs. And so they were. Said Riggs in one commercial: "I wear Hai-Karate After-Shave. That way, the ladies can't concentrate." Meanwhile King heartily endorsed Sunbeam's Mist-Stick Curler-Styler. And, so it went.

Now what makes Bobby Riggs an expert on after-shave lotion or Billie Jean King an expert on curler-stylers escapes me, but the appeals are made nonetheless. That's the way it is in *testimonials:* people who pop into the national spotlight—usually athletes or movie stars—are suddenly experts in many other areas. A glance through any magazine or an hour of television will reveal the following expertise: a golfer on men's pants, a racing car driver on the taste of cigarettes, a baseball player on razors, and so on.

Appeals take many forms. For example, an appeal may be made to an earlier (and therefore "better") age. Phyllis Schlafly, a leading opponent of the Equal Rights Amendment for Women, in pleading her case cites the benefits women receive (without the help of the ERA) from the traditional respect and honor given to Mary, the Mother of Christ. Meanwhile, Gloria Steinem, a leading exponent of the Equal Rights Amendment and the women's liberation movement, invokes a time before the Industrial Revolution when in agricultural societies similar chores were performed by men and women cooperating with one another, working together by day and staying together by night.

Then there is the often used direct *appeal to authority* (as it is called) in which the speaker's opinion becomes associated with the prestige, influence, and reputation of the church, perhaps, or the government, or some expert in a particular field—or all three.

The Bible is used, and the dictionary. The Ten Commandments. The Constitution. The Founding Fathers. For example, before the Japanese attack on Pearl Harbor, the country was seriously divided on whether or not the United States should intervene directly in Europe on behalf of the British and French. Those against such intervention were quick to cite the authority of Thomas Jefferson, who had early in the country's history warned against "entangling alliances."

For better or worse our legal system is based in large measure on citing the authority associated with decisions made in previous cases. And even those in authority appeal to authority. As the American public became increasingly disenchanted with the Vietnam war, presidents invoked the names of their predecessors, the previous president or presidents who had seen fit to sustain our involvement in southeast Asia.

These are just a few examples. The fact is that we need not go beyond our own families and friends to accumulate a rather lengthy list of appeals to authority: even the parents of a friend down the street who allow their son or daughter the use of the family car can become an *appeal to authority*, as can a statement by a favorite instructor who claims to know how we can solve inflation.

Appeals that invoke statistics have a particularly authoritative and seductive appeal. Huff cites an old *New York Times* article which stated that members of the Indianapolis Building Trades Unions received a 5 percent wage increase. This supposedly gave back to the members, the paper reported, one-fourth of the 20 percent wage decrease they had been forced to take earlier. As Huff says, it sounds reasonable but, as it turns out, one-fourth is not an accurate figure: the decrease of 20 percent had been figured on the higher wage the workers had been getting, while the present increase of 5 percent was figured on the lower amount they were receiving (after the cut and before the increase). In other words, says Huff, if the wage before the cut was $1.00 an hour, a 20 percent decrease would cut the hourly wage to $.80. A 5 percent increase on $.80 an hour is $.04, which equals only one-fifth—not one-fourth—of the 20 percent cut they had originally received. And it was in fact a 5 percent increase on the $.80 an hour wage that the workers did receive, not 5 percent of the original $1.00 an hour wage. Thus, the increase amounted to $.04, or one-fifth of the 20 percent ($.20) cut they had taken.

It is simply not the case that "you can prove anything with figures (or statistics) . . ." To the uninitiated it just seems that you can.
—*Lionel Ruby*

Statistics are deceptive even though numbers often seem to possess unimpeachable authority. But any reference to authority designed to break down the reasoning process must not be used as a substitute for our own thinking. Lionel Ruby has wisely advised us to "add to our knowledge and sharpen our critical abilities." Learn to challenge. An unused mind is quick to rust.

Suggestions

◆§ Relate an incident in which a particular appeal by association is made. Recount the incident in your journal and discuss it with the class. What were the circumstances? Who was involved? What was the result? Was the appeal fair or unfair, harmless or harmful? Explain.

◆§ Discuss appeals to authority that you have personally experienced on the campus, on the job, and at home. What was your reaction? Did you challenge the appeal? Why or why not?

◄§   Are there any appeals to authority in this chapter? In the book? If so, point them out and determine what purpose they serve, if any.

◄§   Explain why it would take a 100 percent increase in wages to offset a 50 percent decrease.

Is there any attempt to purposely mislead? Are we seeing only some of the cards while the rest of the deck is held out of sight; that is, are we given all the facts or only some?

Madison Avenue's Samm Sinclair Baker warns that what isn't said is often more important than what is said: "A number of makers of different autos and various brands of gasoline all claim to have won first place in racing and mileage tests; an auto buff explained, 'You want to know how they could all win? Easy. The cars and gasolines may be entered in many races. But they only tell in the ads about the ones they won, not those that came out the wrong way for them. A brand may win in one race and lose in six or seven others, but the ads only mention the win.' "

In a still more serious matter, Baker recounts that in 1966 the Food and Drug Administration took steps to curb the Upjohn Company's advertisements of its new drug, Lincocin. The ads, it seems, emphasized that the drug's side effects would not cause nervous disorder or kidney trouble. What the ads did not stress equally was the fact that use of the drug did sometimes cause blood poisoning and severe diarrhea. Nor did the ad emphasize that doctors should run tests on their patients before writing prescriptions. Too often, the most important facts are left out.

Carefully omitting portions of what someone says or writes in order to twist the speaker's or writer's intended meaning is another undesirable practice, and Baker recounts this example:

> A full-page ad in *The New York Times* for the musical play *Illya Darling* quoted Edwin Newman, critic for the National Broadcasting Company, as saying: "Melina [Mercouri, the show's star] is irresistible." Mr. Newman had actually said: "Illya Darling rests on the premise that Melina Mercouri is irresistible. Even if one accepts this unlikely premise, this is a tasteless, heavy-handed show beyond anyone's capacity to bring to life." The advertiser alibied that the regrettable error was caused by the heat of an advertising deadline. . . .

Of course, as the cartoon here indicates, government can be just

Drawing by Engelhardt; © 1974. *St. Louis Post-Dispatch.*

"No, Don't Classify That One — It's Good News"

as guilty of this kind of deception as individuals. The victim is supplied with facts—but not *all* the facts—a maneuver known as *card stacking.*

The teaching of American history—wittingly or unwittingly—has been a blatant example of not telling all. The "discovery" of America, we were taught, came only with the arrival of the white European to this continent. This "discovery" disregards the fact that for "at least a hundred and fifty centuries before 'Yankee Doodle,' the Indians' way of life composed 'the American way of life.'" Similar disregard continued by denying the contributions made by black Americans.

The 186,000 blacks who fought on the Union side during the Civil War were left out of our history books, just as was Dr. Daniel Hale Williams, the black man who in 1893 completed the first successful open-heart surgery. Admiral Perry's navigator was actually the first man to reach the North Pole; is it because Matt Henson was a black man that we hear nothing of him and only of Perry? There were four black regiments that rode alongside Teddy Roosevelt's Rough Riders to the top of San Juan Hill, but who knows about them? As Bill Cosby has put it: "They didn't get lost going up the Hill; they got lost in the history books."

Suggestions

◄§ Presenting only what favors one's own side in a particular situation is a natural and compelling temptation. Think of a situation in which you gave some of the facts but not all of them to make you or your viewpoint look better. Perhaps you wanted to use the family car, or needed to persuade your instructor that you needed extra time before handing in a paper. (You may have said that you had to work overtime on the job, but you didn't say anything about watching Part I and Part II of a television movie the two nights preceding the deadline date for the paper.)

◄§ Do you know of any situation in which there was an attempt to purposely mislead? If so, describe the circumstances. Who was involved? Who withheld information? What was the result? In your judgment, was the withholding justified? Explain your answer.

What attempts are made to manipulate certain words and phrases to suit a purpose?

Certain words seem to us to carry a high degree of virtue in association with the object or issue in question. For the most part these "virtue words" occur on a high level of abstraction—"beauty," "love," "courage"—and carry a high level of prestige—"the church," "the government."

The use of these words does what much advertising seeks to do: *redefine* products into something new and better. Pepsi-Cola, for instance, has advertised its soft drink in such a way that by now it is hardly a mere liquid; it is, instead, "youth" and "zest" and "joy" overflowing. The drink itself seems almost incidental; it has become instead all the things it is associated with in countless advertisements. By now Pepsi-Cola equals "the good life."

The glitter of particular words and the ability to associate that glitter (in *glittering generalities*) with an individual or group, idea or object, and the ability to connect (or *transfer*, as it is known) power and prestige, wealth and sophistication, with an individual or group, idea or item, is apparent in the accompanying necklace advertisement. Note particularly the words associated with these "mysterious" gems, such as "exotic," "exciting," and "romantic"—all words that glitter. An additional enticement is the promise that the Gallery of Gems can present them *now*, in time for all those "young hearts" who delight in such lovely jewelry.

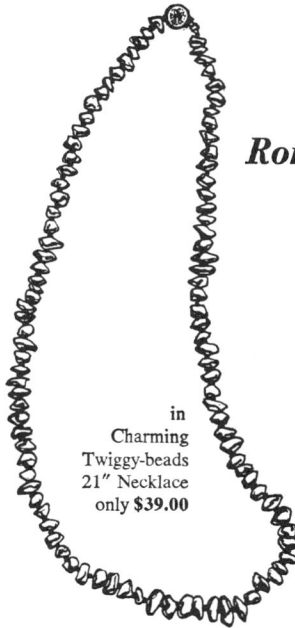

By permission of Louis Zara, Astro Minerals Ltd.

This rare gem, known since "earliest times," was a favorite with "royalty," through the Victorian era and even today. This association of the gems with royalty is an attempt to transfer all the wealth, prestige, and power to the gems themselves. Further associations are made with "meteorites" and the "Apollo 'Moon Rocks.' " Even a link with "Biblical times" is not overlooked.

The qualities we respect, the things we stand in awe of, are frequently transferred to an object that others would have us accept. The Sunoco gasoline advertisements are a good example: "The sun is the greatest source of energy in the solar system. It's fitting that Sunoco takes its name from it." With similar hopes of transfer, one manufacturer of recording tape asserts that if Beethoven were alive today he would be recording his music on Scotch brand tape. (How the company can insist with such certainty what brand Beethoven—deafness and all—would select is not made clear.)

Far more injurious and beyond any sense of fairness are those instances in which words are redefined for unsuitable and even dishonest purposes. In June 1974 Richard G. Kleindienst became the first United States Attorney General convicted of misconduct in office. In April 1971 then president Richard Nixon had personally ordered him as Acting Attorney General to halt antitrust litigation against the huge conglomerate International Telephone and Telegraph Corporation, an intervention by the President that Kleindienst had failed to disclose in hearings before the Senate Judiciary Committee in 1972. Kleindienst had lied.

But in sentencing the former Attorney General to one month in jail (suspended) and a $100 fine (suspended)—the maximum possible was one year in prison and a fine of up to $1000—Judge George L. Hart, Jr., claimed that what Kleindienst had pleaded guilty to was a "technical violation of the law" but was "not the type of violation that reflects a mind bent on deception." Judge Hart added that Kleindienst was a man of "highest integrity."

When questioned by reporters about having concealed from the Committee the fact that the President had urged him to drop the case against ITT (which he refused to do), Kleindienst is reported to have replied that he never felt in his heart that he had perjured himself.

But under oath on March 8, 1972, during the confirmation hearings on his nomination to be Attorney General, Kleindienst had made this statement, taken directly from the *Hearings before the Committee on the Judiciary, United States Senate, Ninety-Second Congress*:

> *Mr. Kleindienst.* Well, I also know this, Senator Kennedy, as

I have testified fully: In the discharge of my responsibilities as the Acting Attorney General in these cases, I was not interfered with by anybody at the White House. I was not importuned; I was not pressured; I was not directed. I did not have conferences with respect to what I should or should not do. So I know that. . . . So, there has been nothing, to my knowledge, based upon my experience and participation or anything that I have heard here that even just by innuendo or conjecture or implication would suggest that in this case there was any improper conduct by anyone or interference, or anything like that.

Discrepencies, it seems, exist in the way Judge Hart has defined "integrity" and "deception" and the way in which others would define them. There may be a discrepency between Kleindienst's definition and the generally accepted definition of what constitutes perjury. And questions might arise about the judge's distinction between a "technical violation of the law" as opposed to any other violation of the law.

Suggestions

◄§ Discuss the use of language in the following advertisement:

If you're a single adult, you know the world is getting bigger and it's getting tougher to find that one great person you'd like to share your world with. Chances are pretty grim of lucking out at work or at some bar and sometimes it seems like all the beautiful people are already married. They're not, you know. We're the scientific matching service you've been hearing about. You're not alone being alone. There are tens of thousands of warm, honest, bright, special people, like you—doctors, stewardesses, engineers, teachers, many others— who would like to find that one special person.

A lot of them are with us. . . . We're not a dating bureau, or an escort service, or a lonely hearts' club. [We're] a space-age concept that puts people together, using psychology, the computer, and human common sense.

Call us for a free personality inventory test. You fill in the empty spaces and we'll go to work to fill in your empty time. Call [us]. We can help.

◄§ Discuss Judge Hart's use of language in suspending the sentence and fine imposed on former Attorney General Richard Kleindienst. Do his definitions of integrity and deception match yours? Do you agree with Kleindienst that he never perjured himself? Can you separate a "technical violation of the law" from a "violation of the law"? Explain each of your answers.

Do you feel that the words have been manipulated, perhaps redefined, in order to suit a particular purpose? Explain your answers.

◄§   Record *in your journal* and bring to class instances you become aware of in which words are manipulated to suit a particular purpose.

◄§   Cite some instances in this chapter in which examples given to illustrate a point under one of the major questions could have illustrated a point under another major question. For example, couldn't the "plain folks" appeal used by Senator Ervin ("I'm an old country lawyer") have served as an illustration of someone's making a claim? That is, isn't Ervin attempting to label himself? Or when Sally jumps to conclusions about who is trying to control her reading, she is leaving something out of the reasoning process, but in doing so, isn't she also seeing a cause and effect relationship where none exists?

     How is it that one example could have been used to illustrate more than one of the basic questions under consideration in this section? What does this overlapping tell you about the nature of language? That is, is language imprecise? Explain your answer.

6 Sexism, Racism and Language

SEXISM AND SEXIST LANGUAGE

Snakes and snails
And puppy dogs' tails,
That's what little boys are made of.
Sugar and spice
And everything nice,
That's what little girls are made of.

So it is established in our early years and so it continues throughout our lives. From the time we hear that "boys will be boys," we are victims of established roles dictated by our society. In *The New Feminism*, a primer on the women's movement, Lucy Komisar quotes twelve-year-old Madeline: "I started German this year. We got a first-grade German book, and suddenly it all came back to me. The first sentence was, 'Mother is shopping, Heidi is painting, and Fritz is flying his airplane.' Everyone is doing what he is supposed to do— of course father isn't mentioned until he comes home from work for supper." (Note, incidentally, Madeline's "proper" use of the pronoun "he" in referring to what "everyone"—even the women— in the family is doing.)

Our experience tells us that when Heidi and Fritz are old enough to attend school, it will be cooking and sewing for her and shop for him. In the same way, people ask little girls about their appearance or their dolls; they ask boys about what they want to be when they grow up. In addition, the mass media do their share and more to reinforce assigned roles. To be a sex goddess, they imply, is every woman's major concern.

Magazines play a part, as a thirteen-year-old in Lucy Komisar's book recalls: "Teen magazines—the teen love and true confessions are terrible. . . . I remember one where a girl who was considered a tomboy was in love with this guy. She got herself some sexy clothes,

119

and he took her out. Then she saved someone from drowning, and he left her! But just as he was leaving, she began to cry, and he came back because *only real girls cry!*"

Perhaps the greatest damage is done in the sex stereotyping that infects children's readers. An analysis of 134 elementary school readers of 14 different publishers used in three New Jersey towns was conducted by the organization Women on Words and Images. From their study, *Dick and Jane as Victims, Sex Stereotyping in Children's Readers*, some startling revelations emerge: in 2,760 stories read in the 134 readers, there were two and one-half times as many boy-centered stories as girl-centered stories; there were three times as many adult male main characters as adult female main characters; and there were six times as many male biographies as female biographies. In addition, women in the stories held 26 different jobs while men held 147, nearly six times as many. The study reports that in these stories women were engaged only in "womanly" occupations—teaching, nursing, and dressmaking. Female jurists or college professors were not to be found.

Not many parents counsel their children to disrupt the established pattern. "I can remember," said a fourteen-year-old in *The New Feminism*, "my mother telling me that it's not good to do things as well as a man does. She said that men don't like it—that men want to win. And if you want to get one, then you have to lose. I said I didn't believe in that, and both my parents replied, 'Well, then you're never going to get married.'"

In this same way, men, too, are victims of a society which insists on their being "masculine"; for a society so steeped in stereotypes of traditional roles of what a "man" will do has little regard for individual differences. The idea of roles is firmly entrenched and amazingly resistant to change. Beth, age fourteen, told in *The New Feminism* of how nervous her high ambitions made some people. Their reactions were so strongly negative that she began to worry that something must be wrong with her. At age nine she decided that she wanted to run for a Senate seat when she was older; a horrified best friend warned that if she dared it would surely interfere with raising her children and caring for her husband. (It is interesting to note that in 1973 the United States Congress granted maternity leave to Representative Yvonne Braithwaite of California, the first such leave *ever* in the nearly two-hundred-year history of that body which represents the people.) And according to the study on children's readers, *Dick and Jane as Victims*, the message is clear from early on: "A young girl is constantly being 'sold' on nursing over doctoring, stenography over business administration, teaching over school administration, and on *motherhood over all other alternatives.* [Italics mine]" Men, on the other hand, are both parents and job holders; women are expected to be one or the other, not both. (It is interesting that in the Education Act Amendment of 1972, designed by Congress to end sex discrimination in schools, from kindergarten through graduate school, an original provision bearing on sexism in textbooks was expressly avoided by the Department of Health, Education and Welfare when it disseminated official regulations enforcing the Act in June 1974.)

Perhaps things are summed up best by another young teenager, Judy, age fifteen: "How can you ever know who your real self is? If you're always playing roles to suit society, then you'll never know."

So, we seem obsessed by our knowledge of who and what we are *supposed* to be. For the males, the word is "masculinity"; for the females, the word is "femininity." What boy is likely, on his own, to ask to enroll in a sewing course, what girl would ask for shop? It's the boy's prerogative to ask for dates, rarely the girl's. Male aggressiveness and dominance are reinforced everywhere. "Don't you like girls?" asked third-grader Caroline Ranold of Lionel (miniature electric toy) Trains President, Ted Bether. "I don't like your ads. Girls like trains too. I am a girl. I like trains . . . Your catalog only has boys." The result: Mr. Bether's promise to get some girls into the advertisements.

The results, however, are seldom so quick in coming; that is, it's going to take more than a letter to change patterns in other areas. From the reaction of today's little leaguer toward his female teammate, to a walk through any office, attitudes about established roles are apparent. What are the chances of seeing an equal number of men and women sitting behind typewriters or holding executive positions?

As Lucy Komisar has said,

> Society tells children from the time they can understand that it is 'masculine' to be an engineer and 'feminine' to be a nurse. It is 'masculine' to be aggressive and 'feminine' to be yielding. When you analyze what is feminine in this society, you discover that it is 'masculine' to control and direct and it is 'feminine' to serve and take orders.

This claim is supported by the reports in *Dick and Jane as Victims*. In children's readers, the study reveals, girls play endlessly with dolls and give numerous tea parties. They look on passively while boys take

Individual differences are far greater than sexual differences.
—*Wilma Scott Heide*

action. On the other hand, boys don't play house, they build houses, while the girls stand aside and admire the results.

In a letter to editors of a Midwestern metropolitan newspaper, a woman proclaimed:

> Bravo to the female former employees of the Edward D. Jones & Co. brokerage house for filing a complaint with the Missouri Human Rights Commission; it seems they were underpaid just because they happened to be born female.
>
> May I point out, however, that Edward D. Jones & Co. was not unique in 1971 (today, too?) among St. Louis brokerage firms in having sexist hiring-personnel policies. Merrill, Lynch, Pierce, Fenner & Smith representatives told me in an interview in January 1971 that certain positions were off-limits to women. Also, female employees there were not allowed to smoke at their desks (no rule for men).
>
> A person need only stand on the observation platform of the New York Stock Exchange trying to spot a female to sense that it is indeed difficult for a woman to break the brokerage barrier.

For the man, the position is that of the "breadwinner"; for the woman, it's the "motherhood mystique." So enormous is the pressure for motherhood that, according to Judith Senderowitz, the first woman president of Zero Population Growth, almost all women in the United States do get married, and after marriage, they are made to feel that they are incomplete human beings if they don't have children. Women find it almost impossible to convey the idea that they simply don't *want* to have children.

What impact does it have on us when we realize that states have laws which declare that if a woman refuses to follow her husband to a new area when he gets a company transfer, she may be declared guilty of abandonment? And what impact did the Michigan food dealers have when they named eighty-one-year-old Ann Koepplinger their "Man of the Year"? What are we being told when of the fifty companies interviewed on the qualities that make for a good executive's wife, not one mentioned intelligence? What is reflected in the following statement by former President Nixon: "I've always found that whenever you find a strong leader, you find a strong woman by his side"?

The part language plays in the perpetuation and reinforcement of arbitrary and often unfair concepts of roles is a major concern. If language perpetuates attitudes, then language can change attitudes. In speaking to the National Organization for Women in 1972, Wilma Scott Heide stated that "when changes are effected, the language sooner or later reflects the change. Our approach is different. Instead of passively noting the change, we are changing language patterns to actively effect the changes, a significant part of which is the conceptual tool of thought, our language."

If the trend toward actual equality for women is a fact, then language should not be a limiting factor. But is it?

Clearly, the English language has reinforced the concept that the woman is a "subspecies" of man. As indicated by the riddle in the *Doonesbury* comic strip seen here, the assumption is that "people," unless specifically identified as women, are men. Our language defines everyone in terms of the male.

Copyright © 1974 G. B. Trudeau / Distributed by Universal Press Syndicate

He is used in situations where both sexes are involved, while both *man* and *mankind* are used to represent everyone; *womankind*, however, carries no such strength.

Aileen C. Hernandez, a past president of the National Organization for Women, states that language indeed "continues to get the message [of male supremacy] across." She points out that, "[T]here is a 'housewife' but no 'housefather'; there's a 'kitchenmaid' but no 'kitchenman'; unmarried women cross the threshold from 'bachelor girl' to 'spinster' to 'old maid,' but unmarried men are 'bachelors' forever."

In fairness, we must point out that not everyone feels oppressed—perhaps not everyone is. Some people assert strongly that they are not. This does not mean, however, that no one is, for certain patterns in our culture are unmistakeable. Psychology Professor Judith Bardwick of Michigan University has sounded this note of warning about new and traditional roles:

> The traditional roles provide fulfillment as well as frustration. And the new roles will provide frustration as well as fulfillment. There are costs and profits in every lifestyle.
>
> I look forward to the day when male and female roles are less arbitrarily divided, when one sex does not automatically have power over the other. In such a culture both sexes will find variety, satisfaction and growth. But from this freedom I am certain that there will emerge a new set of anxieties and crises. The uncertain transition will not be easy. . . .

Still, what propels the Women's Liberation Movement, Gloria Steinem has pointed out, is the quest for meaningful individual choice. Traditional roles are fine for those who want them, but the woman who wants a career as an engineer or truck driver, nuclear physicist or jockey, should not suffer the stumbling block of her sex. Similarly, men who want to keep house, or work as secretaries, or nurses should be able to.

Thus, we need to be aware of established patterns and particularly what part language plays in perpetuating them or can play in changing them. How these patterns change will depend in large measure on how alert we are to the things that will determine those changes. "The brain has no sex," declares Lucy Komisar. "Neither does the heart or mind or soul or whatever it is that makes people want to direct their lives in one direction or another. But there is something that makes one individual want to be a high school teacher, another an engineer, a third a nurse, and a fourth a business executive—and it has nothing whatsoever to do with the nature of his or her genetics. It has to do with culture."

The culture that Komisar speaks of has much to do with language and language has the power we give it. We need to be sensitive to that power.

One individual sensitive to that power is William A. Sutton of Ball State University who sees the clear relationship between improved language alertness and improved treatment of others. His own alertness has led him to suggest the following changes in our presently sexist language:

1. Substitution of an Article for a Pronoun
   Original: "Designed to improve the work of the teacher of piano in *his* handling of class and private instruction."
   Revision: "Designed to improve the work of the teacher of piano in *the* handling of class and private instruction."

2. Substitution of Noun for Nominative Pronoun
   Original: "In major operas or musical productions *he* shares in management or serves as assistant director."
   Revision: "In major operas or musical productions *the student* shares in management or serves as assistant director."

3. Substitution of Possessive Noun for Possessive Pronoun
   Original: "The student will be assigned to a given faculty member, who will supervise *his* classroom activities and assess *his* performance."
   Revision: "A faculty member will be assigned to supervise and assess *the student's* classroom activities and performance."

4. Eliminating the Assumption of Male Identity
   Original: "A specific composer and *his* works, research methods, bibliography and other similar topics may be investigated."
   Revision: "Works, research methods, bibliography, and other similar topics relating to a specific composer may be investigated."

5. Substituting Appropriate Plural Pronoun for Inappropriate Male(s)-Only Pronoun
   Original: "A course designed for the doctoral student which allows *him* to select and explore problems pertinent to art education."
   Revision: "A course designed for doctoral students which allows *them* to select and explore problems pertinent to art education."
   Original: "Familiarizes *the student* with the fine points of Russian grammar and trains *him* to express *himself* in the correct idiom."
   Revision: "Familiarizes *students* with the fine points of Russian grammar and trains *them* to express *themselves* in the correct idiom."
   Original: "The student is encouraged to work with audiotape, videotape, motion picture film, slides, and to assist in the expression of *his* idea."
   Revision: "Students are encouraged to work with . . . and to assist in the expression of *their* ideas."

Suggestions

◄§ Collect some examples of sexist language. Rewrite the sentences eliminating their sexist elements.

≈§   Discuss terms that could be used to eliminate the sexist identification of the titles below. Cite those terms, if you feel there are any, in which the change would be more awkward than helpful. Cite those titles which seem satisfactory to you. Explain your answer.

a) workmen
b) mailman
c) policeman, policewoman
d) aviator, aviatrix
e) chairman, chairwomen, chairperson

Add new items to the list and discuss them.

RACISM AND RACIST LANGUAGE

In 1967 President Lyndon Johnson appointed an investigating committee to find out why racial strife had been erupting nationwide. That committee, The National Advisory Commission on Civil Disorders (referred to as the Kerner Commission), published its findings in 1968.

What the committee concluded should hardly have jolted anyone, but it did. Acknowledging in the Report that "[r]acial violence was present almost from the beginning of the American experience," the commission enunciated the cause: white racism.

The Indian culture, though native to the land, was considered the alien one.
—Knowles/Prewitt

This white racism, which had begun as a movement by the English colonist to "save" the American Indian, culminated three centuries later in the rebellion of black Americans. In the words of the Commission Report, "By 1967 . . . [blacks] could feel the persistent, pervasive racism that kept them in inferior segregated schools, restricted them to ghettos, barred them from fair employment, provided double standards in courts of justice, inflicted bodily harm on their children, and blighted their lives with a sense of hopelessness and despair."

But Louis L. Knowles and Kenneth Prewitt in their book *Institutional Racism in America*, while they agree with the conclusion of the Report that "white racism is essentially responsible for the explosive mixture which has been accumulating in our cities since the end of World War II," are dissatisfied with the "familiar list" of the conditions of the racial strife. "Paraded before the reader," say Knowles and Prewitt, "are observations about the frustrated hopes of Negroes, the 'belief' among Negroes that there is police brutality, the high unemployment in the ghetto, the weak family structure and social disorganization in the Negro community, and so on."

Thus, despite the Report's admission that "white institutions created [the ghetto], white institutions maintain it, and white society condones it," Knowles and Prewitt stress the failure of the Report to deal with *the causes behind the conditions.*

Gouache, 28¾ x 20½". Collection of The Whitney Museum of American Art, New York. Photo, Geoffrey Clements Photography, Staten Island, N.Y.

Tombstones, Jacob Lawrence, 1942

Knowles and Prewitt sum up their feelings: "The recommendations [of the Report] are directed at ghetto conditions and *not* at the white structures and practices which are responsible for those conditions."

Racial mistrust in America—as pervasive as heat inside an oven—has run parallel to the prolonged separation of at least two societies —one black, one white. Insensitivity toward language has reinforced this separation. That insensitivity is discussed in the following article by Haig A. Bosmajian.

THE LANGUAGE OF WHITE RACISM

Haig A. Bosmajian

The attempts to eradicate racism in the United States have been focused notably on the blacks of America, not the whites. What is striking is that while we are inundated with TV programs portraying the plight of black Americans, and with panel discussions focusing on black Americans, we very seldom hear or see any extensive public discussion, literature or programs directly related to the source of the racism, the white American. We continually see on our TV sets and in our periodicals pictures and descriptions of undernourished black children, but we seldom see pictures or get analyses of the millions of school-age white suburban children being taught racism in their white classrooms; we see pictures of unemployed blacks aimlessly walking the streets in their black communities, but seldom do we ever see the whites who have been largely responsible, directly or indirectly, for this unemployment and segregation; we continually hear panelists discussing and diagnosing the blacks in America, but seldom do we hear panelists discussing and diagnosing the whites and their subtle and not so subtle racism.

Gunnar Myrdal, in the Introduction to his classic *An American Dilemma*, wrote that as he "proceeded in his studies into the Negro problem (an unfortunate phrase), it became increasingly evident that little, if anything, could be scientifically explained in terms of the peculiarities of the Negroes themselves." It is the white majority group, said Myrdal, "that naturally determines the Negro's 'place.' All our attempts to reach scientific explanations of why the Negroes are what they are and why they live as they do have regularly led to determinants on the white side of the race line." As the July 1966 editorial in *Ebony* put it, "for too long now, we have focused on the symptoms of the disease rather than the disease itself. It is time now for us to face the fact that Negroes are oppressed in America not by 'the pathology of the ghetto,' as some experts contend, but by the pathology of the white community." In calling for a White House Conference on Whites, the *Ebony* editorial made the important point that "we need to know more about the pathology of the white community. We need conferences in which white leaders will talk not about us (Negroes) but about themselves."

White Americans, through the mass media and individually, must begin to focus their attention not on the condition of the victimized, but on the victimizer. Whitey must begin to take the advice of various black spokesmen who suggest that white Americans start solving the racial strife in this country by eradicating white racism in white communities, instead of going into black communities or joining black organizations or working for legislation to "give" the blacks political and social rights. This suggestion has come from Floyd McKissick, Malcolm X, and Stokely Carmichael. McKissick, when asked what the role of the white man was in the black man's struggle, answered: "If there are whites who are not racists, and I believe there are a few, a *very* few, let them go to their own communities and teach; teach white people the truth about the black man." Malcolm X wrote in his autobiography: "The Negroes aren't the racists. Where the really sincere white people have to do their 'proving' of themselves is not among the black *victims*, but out on the battle lines of where America's racism really *is*—and that's in their own home communities; America's racism is among their own fellow whites. That's where the sincere whites who really mean to accomplish something have to work." Stokely Carmichael, writing in the September 22, 1966, issue of *The New York Review of Books*, said: "One of the most disturbing things about almost all white supporters of the movement has been that they are afraid to go into their own communities—which is where the racism exists—and to work to get rid of it."

A step in that direction which most whites can take is to clean up their language to rid it of words and phrases which connote racism to the blacks. Whereas many blacks have demonstrated an increased sensitivity to language and an awareness of the impact of words and phrases upon both black and white listeners, the whites of this nation have demonstrated little sensitivity to the language of racial strife. Whitey has been for too long speaking and writing in terminology which, often being offensive to the blacks, creates hostility and suspicions and breaks down communication.

The increased awareness and sensitivity of the black American to the impact of language is being reflected in various ways. Within the past two years, there have been an increasing number of references by Negro writers and speakers to the *"Through*

the Looking Glass" episode where Humpty Dumpty says:
"When I use a word it means just what I choose it to mean—
neither more nor less." "The question is," said Alice, "whether
you can make words mean so many different things." "The question is," said Humpty Dumpty, "which is to be master—that's
all." The "Through the Looking Glass" episode was used by
Lerone Bennett, Jr., in the November 1967 issue of *Ebony* to introduce his article dealing with whether black Americans should
call themselves "Negroes," "Blacks," or "Afro-Americans." In a
speech delivered January 16, 1967, to the students at Morgan
State College, Stokely Carmichael prefaced a retelling of the
above Lewis Carroll tale with: "It (definition) is very, very important because I believe that people who can define are mas-
ters." Carmichael went on to say: "So I say 'black power' and
someone says 'you mean violence.' And they expect me to say,
'no, no. I don't mean violence, I don't mean that.' Later for
you; I am master of my own terms. If black power means violence to you, that is your problem. . . . I know what it means
in my mind. I will stand clear and you must understand that
because the first need of a free people is to be able to define their
own terms and have those terms recognized by their oppressors.
. . . Camus says that when a slave says 'no' he begins to exist."
. . . Simon Podair, writing in the Fourth Quarter issue, 1956,
of *Phylon* examines the connotations of such words as "black-
mail," "blacklist," "black book," "black sheep," and "blackball."
The assertion made by Podair that it has been white civil-
ization which has attributed to the word "black" things undesirable and evil warrants brief examination. He is correct when he
asserts that "language as a potent force in our society goes beyond being merely a communicative device. Language not only
expresses ideas and concepts but it may actually shape them.
Often the process is completely unconscious with the individual
concerned unaware of the influence of the spoken or written
expressions upon his thought processes. Language can thus become an instrument of both propaganda and indoctrination for a
given idea." Further, Podair is correct in saying that "so powerful is the role of language in its imprint upon the human mind
that even the minority group may begin to accept the very expressions that aid in its stereotyping. Thus, even Negroes may
develop speech patterns filled with expressions leading to the
strengthening of stereotypes." Podair's point is illustrated by
the comments made by a Negro state official in Washington
upon hearing of the shooting of Robert Kennedy. The Director
of the Washington State Board Against Discrimination said:
"This is a black day in our country's history." Immediately after
uttering this statement with the negative connotation of "black,"
he declared that Robert Kennedy "is a hero in the eyes of black

people—a champion of the oppressed—and we all pray for his complete recovery."

. . . The Negro's increased understanding and sensitivity to language as it is related to them demands that white Americans follow suit with a similar understanding and sensitivity which they have not yet demonstrated too well. During the 1960s, at a time when black Americans have been attempting more than ever to communicate to whites, through speeches, marches, sit-ins, demonstrations, through violence and non-violence, the barriers of communication between blacks and whites seem to be almost as divisive as they have been in the past one hundred years, no thanks to the whites. One has only to watch the TV panelists, blacks and whites, discussing the black American's protest and his aspirations, to see the facial expressions of the black panelists when a white on the panel speaks of "Our colored boys in Vietnam." The black panelists knowingly smile at the racist phrasing and it is not difficult to understand the skepticism and suspicion which the blacks henceforth will maintain toward the white panelist who offends with "our colored boys in Vietnam." "Our colored boys in Vietnam" is a close relation to "our colored people" and "our colored," phrases which communicate more to the black American listener than is intended by the white speaker. John Howard Griffin has pointed out something that applies not only to Southern whites, but to white Americans generally: "A great many of us Southern whites have grown up using an expression that Negroes can hardly bear to hear and yet tragically enough we use it because we believe it. It's an expression that we use when we say how much we love, what we patronizingly call 'our Negroes.'" The white American who talks of "our colored boys in Vietnam" offends the Negro triply; first, by referring to the black American men as "our" which is, as Griffin points out, patronizing; second, by using the nineteenth century term "colored"; third, by referring to the black American men as "boys."

Most whites, if not all, know that "nigger" and "boy" are offensive to the Negro; in fact, such language could be classified as "fighting words." But the insensitive and offensive whites continue today to indulge in expressing their overt and covert prejudices by using these obviously derogatory terms. Running a series of articles on racism in athletics, *Sports Illustrated* quoted a Negro football player as saying: "The word was never given bluntly; usually it took the form of a friendly oblique talk with one of the assistant coaches. I remember one time one of the coaches came to me and said, '(Head Coach) Jim Owens loves you boys. We know you get a lot of publicity, but don't let it go to your head.' Hell, when he said 'Jim Owens loves you boys,' I just shut him off. That did it. I knew what he was talking about." An athletic director at one of the larger Southwestern universities, discussing how much sports have done for the Negro, declared: "In general, the nigger athlete is a little hungrier and we have been blessed with having some real outstanding ones. We think they've done a lot for us, and we think we've done a lot for them" (*Sports Illustrated*, July 1, 1968). One of the Negro athletes said of the coaching personnel at the same university: "They can pronounce Negro if they want to. *They can pronounce it.* But I think it seems like such a little thing to them. The trouble with them is they're not thinking of the Negro and how he feels. Wouldn't you suppose that if there was one word these guys that live off Negroes would get rid of, one single word in the whole vocabulary, it would be *nigger?*" (*Sports Illustrated*, July 15, 1968). When a newspaperman tried to get the attention of Elvin Hayes, star basketball player at the University of Houston, the reporter shouted, "Hey, boy!" Hayes turned to the reporter and said: "Boy's on *Tarzan.* Boy plays on *Tarzan.* I'm no boy. I'm 22 years old. I worked hard to become a man. I don't call you boy." The reporter apologized and said: "I didn't mean anything by it" (*Sports Illustrated*, July 1, 1968).

Whites who would never think of referring to Negroes as "boy" or "nigger" do, however, reveal themselves through less obviously racist language. A day does not go by without one hearing, from people who should know better, about "the Negro problem," a phrase which carries with it the implication that the Negro is a problem. One is reminded of the Nazis talking about "the Jewish problem." There was no Jewish problem! Yet the phrase carried the implication that the Jews were a problem in Germany and hence being a problem invited a solution and the solution Hitler proposed and carried out was the "final solution." Even the most competent writers fall into the "Negro problem" trap; James Reston of the *New York Times* wrote on April 7, 1968: "When Gunnar Myrdal, the Swedish social philosopher who has followed the Negro problem in America for forty years, came back recently, he felt that a great deal had changed for the better, but concluded that we have greatly underestimated the scope of the Negro problem." Myrdal himself titled his 1944 classic work *The American Dilemma: The Negro Problem and Modern Democracy.* A book published in 1967, *The Negro in 20th Century America,* by John Hope Franklin and Isidore Starr, starts off in the Table of Contents with "Book One: *The Negro Problem*"; the foreword begins, "The Negro problem was selected because it is one of the great case studies in man's never-ending fight for equal rights." One of the selections in the book, a debate in which James Baldwin participates, has Baldwin's debate opponent saying that "the Negro problem is a very complicated one." There are several indications that from here on out the black American is no longer going to accept the phrase "the Negro problem." As Lerone Bennett, Jr., said in the August 1965 issue of *Ebony*, "there is no Negro problem in America. The problem of race in America, insofar as that problem is related to packets of melanin in men's skins, is a white problem." In 1966, the editors of *Ebony* published a book of essays dealing with American black-white relations entitled *The WHITE Problem in America*. It is difficult to imagine Negroes sitting around during the next decade talking about "the Negro problem" just as it is difficult to imagine Jews in 1939 referring to themselves as "the Jewish problem."

The racial brainwashing of whites in the United States leads them to utter such statements as "You don't sound like a Negro" or "Well, he didn't sound like a Negro to me." John Howard Griffin, who changed the color of his skin from white to black to find out what it mean to be black in America, was ashamed to admit that he thought he could not pass for a Negro because he "didn't know how to speak Negro." "There is an illusion in this land," said Griffin, "that unless you sound as though you are reading Uncle Remus you couldn't possibly have an authentic Negro dialect. But I don't know what we've been using for ears because you don't have to be in the Negro community five minutes before the truth strikes and the truth is that there are just as many speech patterns in the Negro community as there are in any other, particularly in areas of rigid segregation where your right shoulder may be touching the shoulder of a Negro Ph.D. and your left shoulder the shoulder of the disadvantaged." A black American, when told that he does not "sound like a Negro," legitimately can ask his white conversationalist, "What does a Negro sound like?" This will probably place the white in a dilemma for he will either have to admit that sounding like a Negro means sounding like Prissy in *Gone With the Wind* ("Who dat say who dat when you say dat?") or that perhaps there is no such thing as "sounding like a Negro." Goodman Ace, writing in the July 27, 1968, issue of the *Saturday Review* points out that years ago radio program planners attempted to write Negroes into the radio scripts, portraying the Negro as something else besides janitors, household maids, and train porters. Someone suggested that in the comedy radio show *Henry Aldrich* Henry might have among his friends a young Negro boy, without belaboring the point that the boy was Negro. As Mr. Ace observes, "just how it would be indicated on radio that the boy is black was not mentioned. Unless he was to be named Rufus or Rastus." Unless, it might be added, he was to be made to "sound like a Negro."

. . . Another facet of the racism of the whites' language is reflected in their habit of referring to talented and great writers, athletes, entertainers, and clergymen as "a great Negro singer" or "a great black poet" or a "great Negro ball player." What need is there for whites to designate the color or race of the person who has excelled? Paul Robeson and Marion Anderson are great and talented singers. James Baldwin and Leroi Jones are talented writers. Why must the whites qualify the greatness of these individuals with "black" or "colored" or "Negro"?

. . . The tendency to designate and identify a person as a Negro when the designation is not necessary carries over into newspaper and magazine reporting of crimes. There was no need for *Time* magazine (July 19, 1968) to designate the race of the individual concerned in the following *Time* report: "In New York City, slum dwellers were sent skidding for cover when Bobby Rogers, 31, Negro superintendent of a grubby South Bronx tenement, sprayed the street with bullets from a sawed-off .30 cal. semi-automatic carbine, killing three men and wounding a fourth." *Time*, for whatever reason, designated the race of the person involved in this instance, but the reports on other criminal offences cited by *Time*, on the same page, did not indicate the race of the "suspects." As a label of primary potency, "Negro" stands out over "superintendent." The assumption that whites can understand and sympathize with the Negro's dismay when black "suspects" are identified by race and white "suspects" are not, is apparently an unwarranted assumption, or it may be possible that the whites *do* understand the dismay and precisely for that reason continue to designate the race of the black criminal suspect. To argue that if the race is not designated in the news story then the reader can assume that the suspected criminal is white, is not acceptable for it makes all the difference if the suspect is identified as "a Negro superintendent," "a white superintendent," or "a superintendent." If we were told, day in and day out, that "a *white* bank clerk embezzled" or "a *white* service station operator stole" or "a *white* unemployed laborer attacked," it would make a difference in the same sense that it makes a difference to identify the criminal suspect as "Negro" or "black."

If many Negroes find it hard to understand why whites have to designate a great writer or a great artist or a common criminal as "colored" or "Negro," so too do many Negroes find it difficult to understand why whites must designate a Negro woman as a "Negress." Offensive as "Negress" is to most blacks, many whites still insist on using the term. In a July 28, 1968, *New York Times Magazine* article, the writer, discussing the 1968 campaigning of Rockefeller and Nixon, wrote: "A fat Negress on the street says, passionately, 'Rocky! Rocky!' " As Gordon Allport has written in *The Nature of Prejudice*, "Members of minority groups are often understandably sensitive to names given them. Not only do they object to deliberately insulting epithets, but sometimes see evil intent where none exists." Allport gives two examples to make his point; one example is the spelling of the word "Negro" with a small "n" and the other example is the word "Negress." "Sex differentiations are objectionable," writes Allport, "since they seem doubly to emphasize ethnic differences: why speak of Jewess and not of Protestantess, or of Negress, and not of whitess?" Just as "Jewess" is offensive to the Jews, so too is "Negress" offensive to the Negroes. "A Negro woman" does not carry the same connotations as "Negress," the latter conveying an emotional emphasis on both the color and sex of the individual. *Webster's New World Dictionary of American Language* says of "Negress": "A Negro woman or girl: often a patronizing or contemptuous term."

When the newspaper reporter tried to get the attention of twenty-two-year-old basketball star Elvin Hayes by shouting, "Hey boy!" and Hayes vigorously objected to being called "boy," the reporter apologized and said: "I didn't mean anything by it." In a few cases, a very few cases, white Americans indeed "didn't mean anything by it." That excuse, however, will no longer do. The whites must make a serious conscious effort to discard the racist cliches of the past, the overt and covert language of racism. "Free, white, and 21" or "That's white of you" are phrases whites can no longer indulge in. Asking white Americans to change their language, to give up some of their cliches, is disturbing enough since the request implies a deficiency in the past use of that language; asking that they discard the language of racism is also disturbing because the people being asked to make the change, in effect, are being told that they have been the perpetrators and perpetuators of racism. Finally, and most important, calling the Negro "nigger" or "boy," or "speaking down" to the Negro, gives Whitey a linguistic power over the victimized black American, a power most whites are unwilling or afraid to give up. A person's language is an extension of himself and to attack his use of language is to attack him. With the language of racism, this is exactly the point for the language of white racism and the racism of the whites are almost one and the same. Difficult and painful as it may be for whites to discard their racist terms, phrases, and cliches, it must be done before blacks and whites can discuss seriously the eradication of white racism.

For a long time, probably, and by now, certainly, white racism has harvested black racism; and insensitivity to language—indistinguishable from insensitivity to people—has played an integral part. Awareness of language can be a first strong step toward healing deeply bruised relationships among human beings.

Suggestions

◄§   What in your personal experience causes you to agree with or dispute Bosmajian's claim that "the language of white racism and the racism of whites are almost one and the same"? In your opinion, does this statement apply only to "white" racism? Explain your answers.

◄§   Do you agree that, as Bosmajian says, a person's language is an extension of the person? Explain your answer.

Do you agree with Bosmajian that a step in eradicating racism is to "clean" the language of words and phrases which reflect racism? Explain.

How is an acute lack of sensitivity seen in the reporter's addressing basketball star Elvin Hayes as "boy"? What is your reaction to the reporter's apology and his explanation that he "didn't mean anything by it"? What is your reaction to Bosmajian's use of the term "Whitey"?

◄§   What similarities, if any, do you see in the nature of racist and sexist language? That is, what is this kind of language the result of?

Compare statements on the power of language made by Bosmajian and those he quotes (Carmichael, Podair, and others) with statements made by Aileen Hernandez and Wilma Scott Heide.

Copyright © King Features Syndicate, 1974

⋘ What other phrases can you think of that display racism, both overt and covert, like those mentioned at the end of Bosmajian's essay? For example, what is meant by such statements as, "He's the laziest white person I know"?

⋘ Collect all examples of racist language that you find in the media or daily conversations. For instance, in a televised speech on CBS in December 1973, Senator Proxmire took exception to then President Nixon's early energy saving measures, feeling that they had not been strict enough. Proxmire insisted on immediate gas rationing and said about the hoarding and selling of gasoline that we would have to find ways "to convert the black market into a white market."

⋘ Return to the examples of stereotyping taken from various sources. Which are also examples of sexism? In what ways? Which are also examples of racism? In what ways?

7 Order

Suggestions

🔊 Break into groups of three or four and as a group rearrange the comic strip frames that follow in the order that the group thinks the cartoonists originally gave it. Discuss as a group each move as it is made.

After the group has settled on a particular order, answer the questions on pages 141–2 pertaining to *Hi and Lois.*

🔊 Again in groups of three or four, put the following frames in an order that makes sense.

After the group has settled on an order—or two—turn to page 142 and answer the questions pertaining to *Beetle Bailey*.

◄§   Again in groups of three or four, put the following frames in an order that makes sense to you.

After the group has settled on an order, or two or more, answer the questions pertaining to *Doonesbury*.

Copyright © 1974 G. B. Trudeau / Distributed by Universal Press Syndicate

✑ Questions

Hi and Lois

Did your group put the title frame first? Why? Could it as easily have been the last frame? Explain your answer.

Did your group find frames 5 and 6 (as they are numbered under the frames) interchangeable once an order was pretty well established?

Beetle Bailey

Is there only one "right" order? Explain.

What are the advantages or disadvantages of each possible order? For example, can frame 6 be used as the first frame? To what advantage?

What would happen if frame 4 began the strip? What would happen if frames 3 and 5 were switched, making 5 the initial frame? That is, do you think it is important to the sense of the strip that the frames are ordered according to descending ranks from captain to lieutenant to sergeant?

Did the word "then" in frame 2 help the group to arrange an order?

Doonesbury

What words in particular were an aid to the group in arranging the frames? How? Did the group find *Doonesbury* more flexible in interchanging frames than it did *Hi and Lois* or *Beetle Bailey*? Does the group see this as an advantage or a disadvantage? Why?

◄§ Bring to class two comic strips with all the frames separated. (Cut the frames so that the edges cannot be used to fit the frames together like a puzzle.)

Choose one comic strip that you think has a particularly rigid sequence, that is, a strip that does not fit together in any other order than the way it appeared in the newspaper or magazine.

Choose another that you think has a more flexible order, one in which some of the frames are interchangeable.

Divide into groups of three or four. Each person in the group should in turn present the separated frames of each strip that he or she has chosen and watch, giving no help, while the members of the group rearrange the frames into a sensible sequence or sequences. Then, with the aid of the person whose strips are being used, the group should discuss the conclusion or conclusions reached by the group, paying particular attention to the advantages and disadvantages of the various sequences.

IMPOSED AND NATURAL ORDER

From working with the various comic strips, it should be clear that there is not necessarily a single order that can be imposed on everything that is written. Note, for example, how interchangeable the first three frames of the *Doonesbury* comic strip are.

Order—the particular arrangement of ideas in a piece of writing—usually comes about in one of two ways: it is imposed on what is about to be written, or it grows out of the idea itself—it is discovered.

I call this latter kind of order "natural" because of the way it seems to emerge naturally out of the ideas the writer has in mind. Often we discover this natural order in what we've written after it's thought out or even after it's written.

Imposed order, on the other hand, is based on some external principle and is *not*, like natural order, inherent in the material itself. The principle here is the order of space, and imposes itself on this paragraph:

> I opened my eyes and bottle [of whiskey], then, and took a good pull, shook all over from head to toe, and looked at my room. It was a sunny morning, and though my window faces west, enough light reflected in to make the room bright. A pity: the Dorset Hotel was built in the early eighteen hundreds, and my room, like many an elder lady, looks its best in a subdued light. Then, as now, the one window was dappled with little rings of dust from dried raindrops; the light-green plaster walls were filigreed with ancient cracks like a relief map of the Dorchester [County, Maryland] marshes; an empty beef-stew can, my ashtray, was overflowing butts (I smoked cigarettes then) onto my writing desk—a bizarre item provided by the management; the notes for my *Inquiry*, then in its seventh year of preparation, filled a mere three peach baskets and one corrugated box with MORTON'S MARVELOUS TOMATOES printed on the end. One wall was partially covered, as it is yet, by a Coast & Geodetic Survey map of Dorchester County—not so annotated as it is now. On another hung an amateur oil painting of what appeared to be a blind man's conception of fourteen whistling swan landing simultaneously in the Atlantic during a half-gale. I don't recall now how I came by it, but I know I let it hang through inertia. In fact, it's still over there on the wall, but once while drunk my friend Harrison Mack, the pickle magnate, drew a kind of nude on top of it in crayon. All over the floor (then, not now) were spread the blueprints of a boat that I was building at the time in a garage down by the range lights on the creek; I'd brought the prints up to do some work on them the day before.

Note how in this selection from John Barth's novel *The Floating Opera*, the eyes of the person in bed move from the window to the plaster walls, to the clutter on his writing desk, back first to one wall with a map on it and then to another wall with a painting on it, and finally to the floor covered with blueprints. Though the look we get may seem as haphazard as the appearance of the room itself, it is difficult to argue with the narrator's next statement: "It seems to me that any arrangement of things at all is an order. If you agree, it follows that my room was as orderly as any room can be, even though the order was an unusual one."

This carefully predetermined look at the room is an example of imposed order, an order which moves from point to point, depending on the wishes of the writer.

Order is especially essential in long places of writing since ideas need to be clearly delineated for the reader, particularly when there are many of them. If what is written stretches over several pages, and no order is imposed, it is important that an order be discovered. But even in shorter pieces, order can help shape the material. For example, in this paragraph (from *The Guns of August*) of less than 150 words historian Barbara Tuchman has made certain that the small string of details given below follows an opening controlling statement which imposes itself on those details and helps explain their significance.

> Edward, the object of this unprecedented gathering of nations [for his funeral in 1910], was often called the "Uncle of Europe," a title which, insofar as Europe's ruling houses were meant, could be taken literally. He was the uncle not only of Kaiser Wilhelm but also, through his wife's sister, the Dowager Empress Marie of Russia, of Czar Nicholas II. His own niece Alix was the Czarina; his daughter Maud was Queen of Norway; another niece, Ena, was Queen of Spain; a third niece, Marie, was soon to be Queen of Rumania. The Danish family of his wife, besides occupying the throne of Denmark, had mothered the Czar of Russia and supplied kings to Greece and Norway. Other relatives, the progeny at various removes of Queen Victoria's nine sons and daughters, were scattered in abundance throughout the courts of Europe.

Imagine this paragraph without the controlling sentence, which appears, in this instance, at the beginning. The specifics which expand and explain why Edward VII of England was in a literal sense the "Uncle of Europe," would hardly make sense if they appeared by themselves; by themselves they would have no general relationship or relationship to each other in the reader's mind. In this case, order gives meaning to what is said.

Order emphasizes where emphasis is necessary, and lets the reader know which idea is most important and which is least. Order helps to arrange. But order is not the material itself nor the ideas themselves. If we freeze milk in a bottle, then chip away the bottle, the milk will have the shape of the bottle it was in. But the shape is not the milk; only the ingredients are the milk. The shape is what we have imposed on the ingredients.

Freezing the milk in a paper carton will give the milk a different shape, but the new shape is no more the milk itself than the earlier shape. Only the ingredients are the milk itself, as only the content is the writing. The shape is not the milk; the order is not the writing. Shape, after all, depends on use: milk in a carton is easy to stack but bottles are prettier to look at. Both make milk easier to handle. Each container has its advantages and disadvantages: cartons are harder to open, but bottles can break. Each serves its purpose.

In the same way, order serves its purpose, whether it is imposed or natural. Sometimes writers first impose an order on what they have to say and depend on that order to arrange their ideas. They arrange their ideas and then begin writing. At other times, writers expect that an appropriate order will grow out of what they have to say. They write and discover that a natural order has developed. The content discovers its own order.

But order without meaningful content is of little use; order cannot impose itself on empty space or blossom naturally from a vacuum. And whatever the content, the essential ingredient of any piece of writing is vivid, specific detail.

Look carefully at the details presented of an old fashioned revival meeting being held on the street as James Baldwin describes it in "Sonny's Blues."

> On the sidewalk across from me, near the entrance to a barbecue joint, some people were holding an old-fashioned revival meeting. The barbecue cook, wearing a dirty white apron, his conked hair reddish and metallic in the pale sun, and a cigarette between his lips, stood in the doorway, watching them. Kids and older people paused in their errands and stood there, along with some older men and a couple of very tough-looking women who watched everything that happened on the avenue, as though they owned it, or were maybe owned by it. Well, they were watching this, too. The revival was being carried on by three sisters in black, and a brother. All they had were their voices and their Bibles and a tambourine. The brother was testifying and while he testified two of the sisters stood together, seeming to say, Amen, and the third sister walked around with the tambourine outstretched and a couple of people dropped coins into it. Then the brother's testimony ended, and the sister who had been taking up the collection dumped the coins into her palm and transferred them to the pocket of her long black robe. Then she raised both hands, striking the tambourine against the air, and then against one hand, and she started to sing. And the two other sisters and the brothers joined in.

Notice, for example, how the barbecue cook is described: he is wearing a dirty apron, has reddish and metallic conked hair, and has a cigarette between his lips. Notice, too, the description of the other people present and even the description of the sounds, such as the singing voices and the striking of the tambourine.

The example Baldwin sets is a good one: use details, be specific; whenever you have something to say, help give it purpose by giving it life.

Suggestions

◦§ In a single paragraph (100–150 words) describe a room that interests you. Concentrate on those details that prompted your interest.

◦§ Divide into groups of three or four. Rearrange the sentences in the following paragraphs in the order your group agrees was the intention of the author. The group should discuss the reasons for moving each sentence. Note especially which words were helpful in the arranging process. Have the group consider the following:

Is there more than one possible order?
If so, is this an advantage? Explain.
Is there a main idea? What is it?
How is it supported? That is, is the main idea supported by one example? by several examples? by details?

A

1. The next is mutual stimulation between the two birds that form a pair, as a part of (or a substitute for) the ordinary methods of visual display.
2. The most important is the singer's recognition of, location of and maintenance of contact with its mate.
3. On the basis of both the field data and our aviary studies we can list the function of duetting under four headings in decreasing order of importance.
4. Last and least is mutual reassurance after some disturbance.
5. The third is an aggressive maintenance of the pair's territorial integrity.

—W. H. Thorpe, *Duet-Singing Birds*

B

1. Although there are many inventions that have helped to make man's life easier, the automobile has been the main source of man's advancement beyond himself.
2. Perhaps the biggest psychological basis and compensation for owning an automobile is that the automobile has become an extension of the individual personality.
3. He can conquer hours and thereby lengthen his time of influence.
4. It has become the means by which man is able to actively express his wishes for power and mastery over nature.
5. No longer is he bound to one place or limited to slow, arduous travel.

—Jean Rosenbaum, *Is Your Volkswagen a Sex Symbol?*

C

1. In the seminar one professor, in a sort of chalk talk, showed these manipulators precisely the types of mental manipulation they could attempt with most likelihood of success.

2. In many of their attempts to work over the fabric of our minds, the professional persuaders are receiving direct help and guidance from respected social scientists.

3. What the persuaders are trying to do in many cases was well summed up by one of their leaders, the president of the Public Relations Society of America, when he said in an address to members: "The stuff with which we work is the fabric of men's minds."

4. Several social science professors at Columbia University, for example, took part in a seminar at the University attended by dozens of New York public relations experts.

—*Vance Packard, The Hidden Persuaders*

From your reading, pick out a paragraph; bring it to class with each sentence written on a separate strip of paper. Have the members of the group work the sentences into the original order. The group should also determine any other possible orders that make sense.

Compare the "Table of Contents" with the "Index" of one of your textbooks. Which order is imposed on the material? Which grows out of the material? What are the advantages of each? Which is more useful? Explain.

Return to the description you wrote of a room that interested you. Is there an order to it? That is, did you impose an order on your description before writing it by deciding to move from wall to wall or floor to ceiling? If you didn't impose an order, do you now see a natural order that grew out of the material?

If there is no order, give it one by rearranging your choice of details. If there is an order, describe briefly what the order is.

Pick out one of your longer journal entries. Find its order. What other orders could you have used? Which order do you like best and why? Rewrite the entry, expanding it, following the order you have chosen to give it.

Select a paragraph from Bosmajian's essay "The Language of White Racism." Can you see an order in the paragraph? Is a main idea stated in the paragraph? Does it come at the beginning? The end? How is that main idea supported? What particular words "link" the sentences together? How is the paragraph tied to the paragraph immediately preceding it? How is the following paragraph linked to the one you have chosen?

Bring to class examples of particularly well written, detailed pieces of writing. Read them out loud and have the class comment on them.

Concentrate on a street scene or any small gathering of people, as Baldwin does, and describe not only what you see but what you hear and what you smell. Think about the things that attracted you; then pick those details that will best convey that attraction. Read your description of the scene or gathering and have the members of the class comment on the selection and vividness of your details and the picture they give.

◄§   Take a walk down the block you live on. Describe what you see. Bring your description to class and read it out loud. Have the class comment on how specific and vivid your details are. Will the class know from your reading what season of the year it is or whether you live on a busy street or a relatively quiet one? Will the class know what the dwelling you live in looks like, how far it is from the end of the block, and how it compares with the other dwellings on the block? Will others in the class get an impression of other people who live on the block?

A FINAL WORD

Any proper summing up of this book will not be accomplished in reading the few words written here at the end by the author, but only in the actions of people willing to extend themselves in their efforts to communicate.

This book has attempted to awaken in its readers an awareness of language and its influence on us. Thus, it has been written not just to be read but to be used, not only in the classroom but wherever communication can help.

With the knowledge that we occupy the same small section of the universe, and with the prospect that we may all be parts of the same fragile cell, we must come to realize that language can be used to separate people or to bring them together. Recognizing the power we give language plus the limits it imposes on us is the first step in making us usefully aware of each other.